E. M. Jung-Inglessis

ST. PETER'S

Scala Books

Distributed by Harper & Row, Publishers

Contents

The author, a native of Berlin now residing in Rome, completed her graduate studies at the University of Rome with a doctoral thesis on Michelangelo and Vittoria Colonna between the Reformation and the Counter-Reformation. She also has a degree from the Vatican School of Paleography, Diplomatics and Archivistic Studies. She taught history of civilization at Georgetown University in Washington, D.C., and is now an accredited journalist at the Vatican and a specialized guide. Among her publications are A History of the Holy Years *and a book on* Rome, 2000 Years of History. *Every year she tours several countries, holding a series of lectures on Rome, the Vatican and St. Peter's.*

1. *Cover:* View of the façade and cupola of St. Peter's from Bernini's colonnade. *For the balustrade running above the colonnade, Gian Lorenzo Bernini and his numerous assistants sculpted 140 statues of saints over three meters high, including many popes wearing the papal tiara. His technique was concise, but highly expressive. The statues seem to be at the mercy of the wind, with their animated gestures and moving drapery, the vision of a majestic "heavenly court" whose scenographic effect is impressive, soul stirring. Poised over the semicircular colonnade, they enshrine the basilica façade dominated by Michelangelo's "Cupolone". Towering above the façade are colossal statues (5.70 m.) of the Savior, John the Baptist, and the eleven apostles chosen by Christ after Simon Peter.*

2. *Frontispiece:* The Papal tiara. *The triple crown, symbol of the papacy, signifies the three states of the Church governed by the Pope, Vicar of Christ: the church militant on earth, penitent in Purgatory, and triumphant in Paradise.*
This splendid 18th-century example of the jeweller's art is kept in the Treasure Museum of St. Peter's. During solemn ceremonies each year on June 29th, St. Peter and St. Paul's feastday, it is used to crown the bronze statue of the Prince of Apostles, in the basilica. It reproduces on a large scale (54 cm. high, 30 cm. in diameter) the tiara used by popes until recent times for their enthronement, during pontifical mass, and on other solemn occasions.

© COPYRIGHT 1980 by SCALA, Istituto Fotografico Editoriale, Firenze
Text: Eva-Maria Jung Inglessis
Editorial Director: Francesco Papafava
Editing and captions: Laura Draghi
Layout: Fried Rosenstock
Translation: Graham Fawcett (text) and Carol Wasserman (captions)
Produced by SCALA, Istituto Fotografico Editoriale
Plans: SCALA
Photographs: SCALA (Mauro Sarri), except: n. 12, Alinari; n. 26, 36, 49, Attualità Fotografica Giordani; n. 5, 7, 9, 16, 24, Biblioteca Apostolica Vaticana; n. 21, British Museum (John Freeman); n. 26, Carrieri; n. 27, 40, 41, 56, 59, 64, 95, Del Priore; n. 27, 28, Felici; n. 8, Istituto Nazionale di Archeologia e Storia dell'Arte di Palazzo Venezia; n. 73, 85, Musei Vaticani; n. 25, 33, 42, 45, 62, 65, 86, Musei Vaticani (Carrieri); n. 71, 92, Nicolini; n. 37, 90, 91, 94, Reverenda Fabbrica di S. Pietro; n. 11, Staatliche Museen Preussischer Kulturbesitz
Printed in Italy by Sogema Marzari S.p.A., Schio, 1980

3

The Old St. Peter's

3. The Vatican at the end of the 15th century. *Xylograph from a book by Hartmann Schedel (1493) showing St. Peter's churchyard with the Benediction* Loggia *and the bell-tower, the walls, the Papal Palace to the right and, beyond, the* Palazzetto del Belvedere.

In mediaeval times the Vatican was a city and a world apart, outside the walls of Rome and across the Tiber. There was a single bridge leading to St. Peter's: the one built in 133 by the Emperor Hadrian (76-138) and called *Ponte Sant'Angelo*, after Gian Lorenzo Bernini's 1667 addition of ten baroque angels each holding a different symbol of Christ's Passion. On the other bank towers the formidable Castel Sant'Angelo, once the mausoleum of the Emperor Hadrian, then a fortress of the popes for the protection of the Vatican.

A big gate next to the castle could open or seal off access to the Vatican. A 600-meter escape route ran along the top of the Leonine Walls, built by Pope Leo IV (847-855), by which the popes were able in time of war to pass directly from the papal palace to safety in Castel Sant'Angelo. Two narrow streets, running parallel, led through the *Borgo*, a built-up quarter of small dwellings, to St. Peter's Square. The square itself was then an irregular rectangle. To the right was a bell-tower and a benediction *Loggia*, or balcony. Thirty-five steps led up from the square to the atrium before the basilica.

There were three doors into this porch area (62 × 56 m) surrounded by columns in the style of an antique *quadriporticus* (like the one still to be seen in St. Paul's Outside the Walls). Here pilgrims encamped, the poor were given food and merchants sold religious articles and souvenirs. Along the walls were the tombs of the famous, such as the porphyry sarcophagus of the German Emperor Otto II (955-983). To the right was the papal palace and to the left the residence of the canons.

In the center of the atrium stood a high ancient fountain in form of a gilded pine-cone out of which water poured from all sides. This was the famous

5

4

5.   St. Peter's Square in 1585. *This fresco by Cesare Nebbia, in the* Salone Sistino *of the Vatican Library, shows che coronation of Sixtus V, with the old buildings of St. Peter's still standing and the new ones under costruction. From left to right are the new Palace of the Inquisition; the archpriest's house, with its open gallery; the entrance to the atrium containing three doors; the three-story Benediction Loggia; the Vatican entrance and the sun-dial above; and the west wing of the Apostolic Palace with the Loggias of Bramante and Raphael. In the background, the bell-tower and gable end of the old basilica are already keeping company with the drum of Michelangelo's* Cupolone *and the smaller Gregorian cupola by Giacomo della Porta (1584).*

4.   The portico and façade of Old St. Peter's. *In this early 17th century drawing by Domenico Tasselli, the old basilica has an open, four-sided atrium with a surronding portico, originally called "The Garden of Paradise". The only remaining late Middle Age structures were the part of the portico beneath the façade and, in the center, the gilded bronze fountain, shaped like a gigantic pine-cone, now in the* Cortile della Pigna *of the Vatican Museums. The 13th-century façade has a mosaic of the same date representing Christ in glory with Pope Gregory IX, who commissioned the work, St. Peter, St. Paul and the Evangelists and, at the bottom, the Elders of the Apocalypse.*

cantharus, the fountain for the ablutions where the pilgrims had to clean and refresh themselves before they entered the house of God.

Only from the atrium was it possible to see the church façade, decorated with mosaics, gleaming golden in the morning sun, since the church faced east: *ex oriente lux*, from the east comes the light. There were five entrance doors to the old St. Peter's: three serving the central nave (*porta ravenniana, mediana, romana*), one opening into the first lateral naves to the left and another to the right (*porta iudicii, porta guidonea*), this last being the way in for guides and groups. The two outer naves did not originally have separate entrances, and only for the

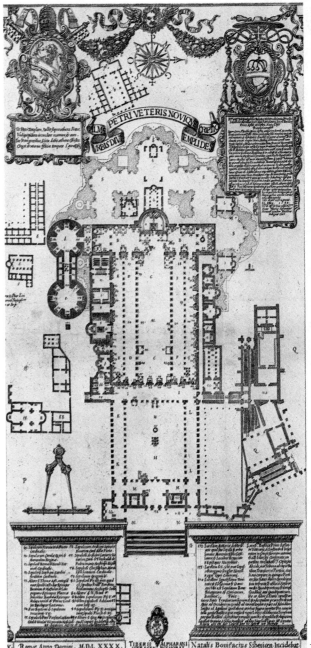

6. The interior of Old St. Peter's. *This Raphael school fresco in the Papal Palace (Hall of Constantine) shows Constantine's legendary Donation. The Emperor gives to the Pope — Sylvester I with the features of Clement VII — the statue of the Goddess Rome, and with it the city. In the background is the papal altar, and the grating from which St. Peter's tomb was visible.*

7. Plan of Old St. Peter's. *The author, Tiberio Alfarano (1594-96), a clerk of the Basilica, was witness to the demolition of the old edifice and the construction of the new one, and wrote an important commentary on the subject. The Rotunds of St. Petronilla and St. Andrew to the left were Imperial mausolea from the age of Theodosius I (347-395).*

Holy Year in 1500 was a Holy Door created on the extreme right hand, to be used only during such solemn occasions every 25 years.

When the pilgrim, after this long gradual approach, finally entered the church, he may well have stopped momentarily in the doorway, or dropped to his knees, overcome with awe and apprehension at its sheer size and magnificence. St. Peter's was in fact the largest and most beautiful church in the world. It had been built soon after the Edict of Milan (313) by which the Emperor Constantine (280-337) conceded to Christians freedom of worship. It is told that the Emperor himself initiated the construction of the church by carrying twelve baskets of earth on his back. In 326 the church was solemnly consecrated by Pope Sylvester I (314-335), probably in the Emperor's presence, although the decoration of the interior was completed only by his son Constans (320-350).

The church was built in the typical shape of a Roman basilica, a long-stretched, right-angled empty hall (118 × 64 m), divided into five equally long naves by 88 Corinthian columns. These four lines of columns directed the eyes of the visitors up to the altar standing between the transept and the apse at the other end of the basilica. The walls were decorated with

8

8. The Adoration of the "Holy Face". In this 15th-century xylograph, the faithful kneel before Veronica's veil (the Volto Santo *or Holy Face) shown from a pulpit. In it, they could make out Christ's features, which were impressed in the cloth when He wiped his blood-and-sweat-covered face on it. It was said that the donor of the* Volto Santo *to the Emperor Tiberius (42 B.C. - 37 A.D.) was Veronica herself (yet her historical authenticity is uncertain). Today this relic is in the* Loggia *of Veronica's Pillar.*

tinus victor tibi condidit aulam. ('As it was with Your guiding hand that he exalted the world to the heavens by his triumph, Constantine the victor built this house for You').

The apse too was decorated with mosaics by Constantine's son Constans and later restored by Innocent III di Segni (1198-1216). It showed Christ with Peter and Paul and the *Ecclesia Romana* personified, between the heavenly Jerusalem and Bethlehem. The transept (86.97 × 17.39 m), which extends beyond the two outer naves for about ten meters on each side, gives the lay-out of a building in the shape of a capital T (a Greek *'tau'*), to be taken as a cross.

As the centuries passed, the appearance of Constantine's basilica was transformed by the addition of a large number of side-chapels, as well as gothic windows and about a hundred new altars. The church was further filled with images of saints, statues, gilded furnishings, silk hangings and oriental tapestries. The interior was always veiled in a magic, mystical gloom, illuminated only by candles and oil lamps. From the lamps clouds of incense and oriental aromas rose up together with the glimmering light. In the Middle Ages, however, the value of the church did not reside in its artistic treasures (as would be the case later on) but in its relics. This sacred edifice housed the most precious relic in existence in the Western world: the bones of St. Peter. As time went on, other relics were added: the head of Andrew the Apostle, Peter's brother, solemnly carried to Rome from Patras in Greece in 1460, and given back to the Greeks with equal ceremony in 1962; a fragment of the Holy Cross, discovered, according to legend, by St. Helen, the mother of Constantine; the point of the lance Longinus used to pierce Christ's side, this being a gift from the Sultan Bajazet II to Innocent VIII Cybo (1484-92) in 1492. But the object which aroused the greatest veneration was Veronica's veil (or *Volto Santo*) bearing Christ's features, impressed on it during Christ's walk to Mount Calvary.

frescoes representing popes as well as scenes of the Old and New Testament. What the interior looked like can still be seen from a fresco called "Constantine's Donation" by the Raphael school in the Hall of Constantine (Pontifical Palace).

From this painting, one can also get an idea of the appearance of Peter's funeral monument as it was at the end of the Middle Ages before the demolition of Old St. Peter's. It consisted of a big square block of marble and was surrounded by twelve twisted columns in white marble, forming a kind of *'pergola'* and was called by that name. On top of the monument was the papal altar, which Sixtus IV della Rovere (1471-84) had rebuilt in about 1475 with four porphyry columns supporting a marble canopy. Visible beneath the altar is a grating: the *fenestella confessionis*, through which the faithful could look into a lower, dark vault in which they believed that the remains of the Apostle lay. But they did not dare penetrate any further for fear of disturbing the peace of the dead saint.

At the end of the central nave, almost over the tomb, a triumphal arch was erected with a splendid mosaic portraying Constantine as the donor. Underneath was a proud inscription: *Quod duce te mundus surrexit in astra triumphans, hanc Constan-*

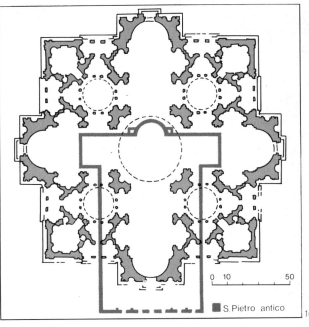

9

10

The building of the New St. Peter's

9. Medal with St. Peter's by Bramante, *executed in 1506 by Caradosso, today in the Vatican Library.*

10. Plan by Bramante, *from anonymous original drawing (Florence, Uffizi) completed here.*

For 1,200 years the Constantine basilica had withstood attacks from Barbarians, Saracens, imperial armies and factions among the nobility. But in the year 1506 Julius II della Rovere (1503-13), dubbed "the dreadful old man", decided with a drastic gesture to demolish this, the most revered church of Christendom. It was certainly an unsafe building whose foundations were shifting, but why could it not have been renovated? A restoration program had in fact already been put in hand by Nicholas V Parentucelli (1446-55). Spurred on by a survey of Leon Battista Alberti's on the bad state of the building, he first projected an enlarged tribune (apse) and then resolved to have the whole church reconstructed. His architect, Bernardo Rossellino, drafted a plan which, however, did not contain a radical rethinking of the design of the original basilica. The foundation of the walls of Rossellino's tribune had been barely laid when Nicholas V died, and the whole building plan was shelved for 50 years.

Only under Julius II was it taken up again. He wanted a modern, light, spacious, elegant church in keeping with the new spirit of the Renaissance, and one which would have to surpass all the buildings of antiquity in size, beauty and harmony. On April 18,

1506, Julius II della Rovere laid the first stone of the new structure on the exact spot where the pilaster of Veronica now stands. To raise the funds needed for the construction, Julius II and his successor Leo X issued indulgences ("*Il grande perdono della Reverenda Fabbrica di San Pietro*") which were sold also in Germany and aroused the famous protest of Martin Luther. Against this commerce of indulgences he wrote his 95 theses "On the value of indulgences", which provoked the outbreak of the Protestant Reformation. Thus a tragic connection exists between the new St. Peter's, which was supposed to be the visible sign of unity and universality of the Church, and the outbreak of the most dramatic schism in the history of Christianity.

Julius II commissioned Donato Bramante with the construction of the new church. In order to get the building materials he needed, Bramante plundered the antique Forum of Rome and turned the entire city into a marble quarry, thus earning the nickname "*Mastro Ruinante*" (Master Ruiner). His plan was for a church in the form of a Greek cross with a cupola over the point of intersection of the two arms, of equal length. It was as though he wanted to put the dome of the Pantheon on top of the basilica of Maxentius. By the time Bramante died, in 1514, on-

11. Interior of New St. Peter's, under construction. *Marten van Heemskerck, a Dutchman living in Rome in 1534-41 made various sketches showing the progress of construction work on St. Peter's. Here the central nave is still standing, its powerful connecting arches rising from four pillars. Above the papal altar is the "tiburio", a provisory protective structure, by Bramante.*

12. Wooden model for St. Peter's. *Now in a storage room in St. Peter's, it was made by Antonio da Sangallo (1534-41). It has a monumental three-nave basilical plan. Michelangelo criticized it because, unlike Bramante's spacious plan, it was "without light", and full of dead-end corners where all sorts of criminals might hide.*

13. Raphael's project. *In this chiaroscuro painting by Giulio Romano (Hall of Constantine, Papal Palace), dated 1520-30, Constantine shows Pope Sylvester I — with the face of Clement VII — the plan of the first basilica. In fact this is the plan submitted by Raphael, Giuliano da Sangallo and* fra *Giocondo to Leo X in 1514.*

14. Construction work on New St. Peter's. *On the right of the preceding painting, realistic details of the construction yard for New St. Peter's. In a letter of the period Raphael writes: "In honoring me, our holy master has placed a great weight on my shoulders. I hope not to fall beneath it…"*

ly the four huge pilasters had actually been put up, which were, together with their connecting arches, 45 m high and were intended to support the cupola. However much Bramante's successors might modify his original plan, it was no longer possible to ignore the fact that these four pilasters were in place, as the legacy from Bramante. On the foundation walls of Rossellino's tribune, Bramante drew up a provisional choir and over the papal altar he constructed a rectangular building for its protection, called *il tiburio*, as can be seen from the sketches done by the Dutch painter Marten van Heemskerck in about 1535.

Bramante was followed by three artists working together: Raphael, Giuliano da Sangallo and Fra Giocondo; this triumvirate submitted to the Pope a design based on the Latin cross. Then Antonio da Sangallo the Younger took charge of the building works in collaboration with Baldassarre Peruzzi. Peruzzi wanted to go back to Bramante's Greek cross, but Sangallo decided on the basilical ground-plan and further amplified it by adding rooms, corridors, chapels and towers. His model in wood is preserved in one of the side rooms of the cupola. Michelangelo deplored these deviations from

13

14

Bramante's original scheme, which he described as *"chiara, schietta, luminosa e isolata attorno"* (clear, pure, light and isolated all around), and accused the entire Sangallo family, "the Sangallo sect", as he referred to them, of having "deviated from the truth", of squandering public funds and wasting valuable time. The work went on slowly, and already weeds were sprouting on the new walls, as Heemskerck showed in his sketches. To the ruins of the old St. Peter's, the ruins of the new were being added.

Antonio da Sangallo raised the floor of the new building by about 3 meters and in 1538 constructed a wall ten meters high between the eleventh and twelfth columns to hide the work site area, so that religious functions could continue unhindered in the front part of the old church left standing for some 70 more years. In 1608 this part was demolished as well. This was the situation when Sangallo died in 1546 and Michelangelo, who had seen the building going up and followed its development with a critical eye

15

and outspoken disapproval, took over as chief of works at more than 70 years of age. "It was not of my willing that I built St. Peter's, and I have always rendered service not only gratis but at great pain and personal discomfort"; but he did it "to the glory of God, in honor of St. Peter and for the salvation of my soul".

The administrators and donors were shocked when they saw that Michelangelo's first step was to knock down almost everything which Sangallo had added to Bramante's beginnings. He then reduced the ground plan by 12 meters, thus "diminishing its size, but increasing its greatness", as Vasari stated. He therefore went back to the idea of a central structure, of a Greek cross, with a big cupola in the middle and four smaller cupolas over the corner chapels. Each cross-arm was to end with an apse, except for the first which was supposed to have a portico as entrance. A fresco by Cesare Nebbia and Giovanni Guerra in the Vatican Library gives us an idea of how the overall architectural effect would have looked; but it is based on mere supposition, because there are neither sketches nor written indications of how Michelangelo might have conceived the façade and the square in front of the church. He did obtain a written assurance (*Motu Proprio*, 1549) from Pope Paul III Farnese (1534-49) that he could build and

demolish at his own discretion, and that his design would be carried out without alterations even after his death.

When Michelangelo died in 1564, only the southern part of the church, the left-hand cross-nave with the apse, had been completed; this part he had done with all details, so that these walls with their rhythm of curved and plain lines, pilasters, windows, niches, capitals and tympanums could serve as a blueprint for the other parts. He had also finished the drum of the cupola. But the most difficult task had yet to be accomplished: the raising up of the vault of the dome.

Michelangelo's successors, Pirro Ligorio and Giacomo Barozzi, known as *il Vignola*, did not dare venture upon such an undertaking. Only 26 years later, despite widespread fear and apprehension, was the cupola completed, thanks to the dogged insistence of Pope Sixtus V Peretti (1585-90), by the architects Giacomo Della Porta and Domenico Fontana.

The church, however, was still not finished. It took the energy and generosity of yet another pope, Paul V Borghese (1605-21), who concentrated every effort on the completion of St. Peter's. But he adjudged Michelangelo's design to be on too small a scale. For the nascent Counter-Reformation, which aimed to emphasize the grandeur of the Roman Church by

15. New St. Peter's, under construction. *In this drawing by Marten van Heemskerck, the part of the Constantinian basilica still standing at the end of the 15th century. One of the tortile columns can be seen from a central window. The old naves have been closed off by a wall built in 1538.*

16. St. Peter's, as planned by Michelangelo. *This fresco, in the Vatican Pinacotheca, painted by Cesare Nebbia in about 1590, shows a front view of the semispherical dome. The church has a projecting frontage with columns, and back and side colonnades. This is only the painter's supposition, for Michelangelo left no documents about it.*

17. Michelangelo gives Pius IV a model of St. Peter's. *The model in this painting (Florence, Casa Buonarroti) is freely rendered by the painter, Donato Cresti, called "il Passignano". Michelangelo, aged nearly 90, believed it impossible to modify his project after he died, having obtained written assurance from Pope Paul III and his successors. Although embittered and weary, he wouldn't abandon this job, "...For I am old, and can leave nothing more of myself... and I do this service for God, and in Him I place all my hope".*

18

outward and visible signs, and for the new Baroque age with its predilection for superb ceremonial and long processions, a church with a longer nave was clearly called for. What was more, the whole floor area of the old basilica, being consecrated ground, needed to be covered over by the new building. There was also a theological argument put forward: the Greek cross was felt to be too Oriental, whereas the Latin cross was more in keeping with the historical reality of the cross of Christ and with Western tradition. So Carlo Maderno was given the task of making the church at least another 60 meters longer. In order to achieve this, the remaining part of the old basilica, with its precious columns and gilded mosaics, was ruthlessly destroyed. The Romans witnessed this fresh act of vandalism in horror, and the archivist Jacopo Grimaldi wrote in desolation on November 15, 1609, in his diary: "This is the last Mass being celebrated in the old basilica".

Besides making a longer nave, Maderno added a large portico and the façade, on which Paul V, in 1612, had his name inscribed, although prematurely because only his successor, Urban VIII Barberini, (1623-44), could finally consecrate the new church on November 18, 1626, exactly 1,300 years after the first basilica was supposedly inaugurated by Sylvester I.

It was the same Urban VIII who called upon Gian

18.   Southwest side of New St. Peter's. The south transept (on the right) is in the area where the Rotunda of St. Petronilla once stood. It alone had every detail specified by Michelangelo, to avoid any future alteration of the other apses. On the left is the central apse. The succession of curvilinear and rectilinear elements, of blind windows and large light-filled openings between the powerful pilaster strips crowned with corinthian columns, and the strong rhythmic movement of the trabeation supporting the attic, give the building a majestic elegance. The vertical emphasis of the lower story, optically increased by the groups of three narrow superimposed niches, contrasts with the horizontal movement of the attic, emphasized by the beautiful rectangular windows.

Lorenzo Bernini to decorate the interior, greeting him with the words: "It is your good fortune, Cavaliere, to have Cardinal Maffeo Barberini as your pope; but we are even more fortunate that there is a Cavaliere Bernini during our Pontificate". With Bernini, the "golden age" of Rome found its climax. It was a time of geniuses. It was their miracle that a building on which so many different hands and minds had worked for over 100 years nevertheless became a harmonious, unitary work of art.

19

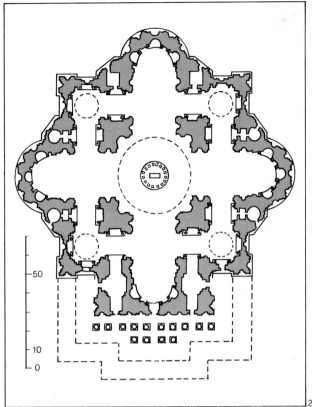

20

19. The apse seen from the gardens. *In Michelangelo's project, the dome of St. Peter's was to be visible from every side, but it is now only from the heights of the Vatican hills. The complete view is cut off by Maderno's construction on the façade side. St. Peter's church was built in the typical Roman travertine, a porous calcareous stone which hardens with time and takes on a clear, ivory-white to rose-grey colored patina.*

20. Plan of Michelangelo's project. *There is no surviving original plan for New St. Peter's by Michelangelo. This one comes from a plan by Martino Ferraboschi (1612), based on the south transept constructed under the direction of Michelangelo, who had returned to Bramante's central plan, which he deemed perfect. He was for a church in the form of a Greek cross with arms of equal leght, each ending in an apse, and a powerful cupola above it at the very center. Around the four pillars supporting the cupola is a wide passageway that leads to the four corner chapels, which are surmounted by smaller cupolas.*

21. Maderno's façade with the towers in his plan. *It seems that Michelangelo meant to built a portico with a double row of columns, and no bell-tower. But Carlo Maderno, between 1607 and 1612, plan-*

21

ned for a closed atrium with a long façade ending in a tower on each side, so as to enshrine the cupola and create a more vertical structure. His idea is illustrated in this print from a book by Martino Ferraboschi (1612). Work on the two towers began in 1612, but insuperable technical difficulties caused its suspension. The towers bore too heavily on the façade, and it threatened to collapse. Gian Lorenzo Bernini again ventured this difficult task, and completed the right-hand tower on St. Peter's day, 1614. But only a few days later he had to demolish part of it, thereby getting himself a sharp reprimand from Pope Urban VIII for his failure.

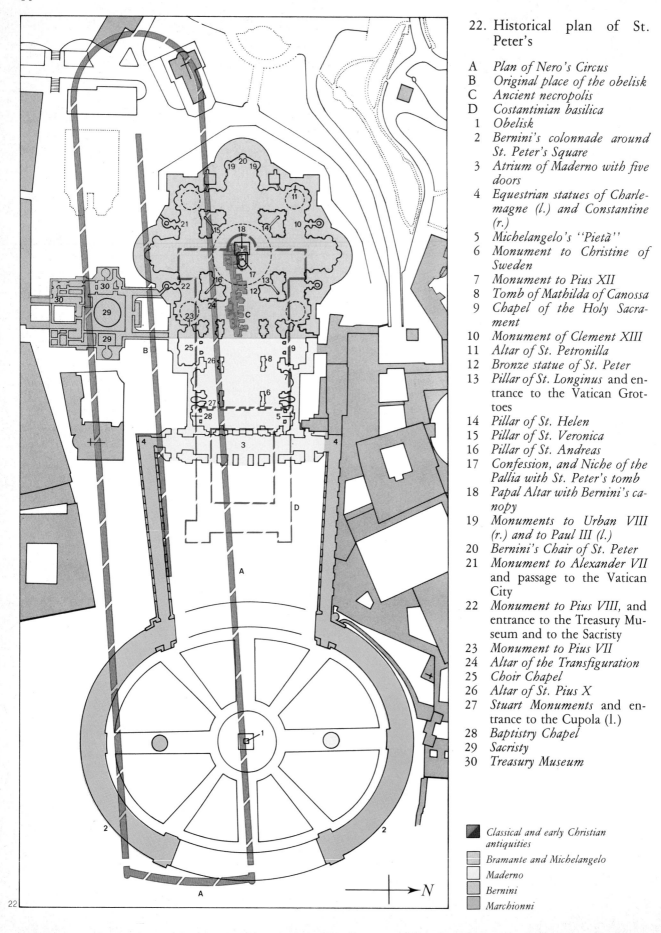

22. Historical plan of St. Peter's

A   *Plan of Nero's Circus*
B   *Original place of the obelisk*
C   *Ancient necropolis*
D   *Costantinian basilica*
1   *Obelisk*
2   *Bernini's colonnade around St. Peter's Square*
3   *Atrium of Maderno with five doors*
4   *Equestrian statues of Charlemagne (l.) and Constantine (r.)*
5   *Michelangelo's "Pietà"*
6   *Monument to Christine of Sweden*
7   *Monument to Pius XII*
8   *Tomb of Mathilda of Canossa*
9   *Chapel of the Holy Sacrament*
10   *Monument of Clement XIII*
11   *Altar of St. Petronilla*
12   *Bronze statue of St. Peter*
13   *Pillar of St. Longinus and entrance to the Vatican Grottoes*
14   *Pillar of St. Helen*
15   *Pillar of St. Veronica*
16   *Pillar of St. Andreas*
17   *Confession, and Niche of the Pallia with St. Peter's tomb*
18   *Papal Altar with Bernini's canopy*
19   *Monuments to Urban VIII (r.) and to Paul III (l.)*
20   *Bernini's Chair of St. Peter*
21   *Monument to Alexander VII* and passage to the Vatican City
22   *Monument to Pius VIII,* and entrance to the Treasury Museum and to the Sacristy
23   *Monument to Pius VII*
24   *Altar of the Transfiguration*
25   *Choir Chapel*
26   *Altar of St. Pius X*
27   *Stuart Monuments* and entrance to the Cupola (l.)
28   *Baptistry Chapel*
29   *Sacristy*
30   *Treasury Museum*

Classical and early Christian antiquities
Bramante and Michelangelo
Maderno
Bernini
Marchionni

→ *N*

23

St. Peter's Square

23.   St. Peter's church and square (aerial view). *St. Peter's church and square are the meeting place of innumerable pilgrims, who travel from all continents to venerate the heart of Christianity, where Peter, first Vicar of Christ, confessed his faith in blood.*

Bernini's most brilliant achievement was St. Peter's Square. He conceived the idea in a completely original way, since neither classical antiquity nor the Middle Ages could have given him his model. Despite the huge dimensions of the elliptical space (198 × 148 m), one does not feel lost in it but protected by two colonnades, which seem to welcome all comers in a majestic embrace. Originally Bernini wanted to enclose the square completely, with a third, shorter series of columns on the east. The impression would have been even stronger for anyone emerging from the labyrinth of little alleys of the Borgo, coming all of a sudden upon the vastness of the square and unexpectedly facing the church in all its splendor. Instead of the colonnade, a gray line of granite now marks the end of the square, and with it the borderline of the Vatican State.

The colonnades comprise 284 travertine columns 16 m high, with Doric capitals, the most severe form of

pillars, arranged in four semi-circular curves whose circumferences increase towards the outer edge in such a way that the distance between one column and another is always the same. From the focal points in the square (there are two, the square being in the form of an ellipse) only the first curve is visible, concealing as it does the three outer ones quite perfectly and giving a highly skillful perspective effect. In addition to the granite discs marking these focal points, the pavement also contains the signs of the zodiac and of the wind rose.

On top of the columns are 140 statues of saints measuring 3.20 m high, by Bernini and his pupils. Between them appear repeatedly the coat-of-arms of Pope Alexander VII Chigi (1655-67) during whose pontificate the square was built.

An obelisk stands exactly in the middle of the great ellipse. Its history of 4,000 years is extraordinary. Erected by Pharaoh Nencores about 1935 B.C. in

Heliopolis, it was transferred in 30 B.C. by the prefect Caius C. Gallus to the Forum of Alexandria. Emperor Caligula had it transported to Rome in 37 A.D. in a ship specially built for the purpose of carrying this 25 meter-long, 327 ton monolith. He erected the obelisk in the center of the circus he had had built for his entertainment on the slope of the Vatican Hill. The circus was inherited by Nero and became known as *Circus Gai et Neronis*. Here, and in the gardens round about, the first mass executions of Christians took place (Tacitus *Annals*, XV, 44) probably in the autumn of 64. The obelisk is therefore an "eyewitness" of the tragic and heroic dawn of Christianity in Rome. It even remained in position long after the circus had been destroyed and the basilica of St. Peter's had been built to the right of it, while chapels and hospices went up on every side. The most recent soundings have revealed the foundations of the obelisk and the circus track at a depth of 20-34 meters. Thus the position of the circus, long disputed, was established, its length being about 500 m from east to west and its breadth about 95 m.

In 1586 Domenico Fontana, upon the order of Sixtus V, succeeded in something which even Michelangelo had considered impossible. He removed the "*guglia*", as the obelisk was then called, from the south side of the basilica to the center of the new square. The undertaking is depicted in another of the Vatican Library frescoes. It needed 900 men, 140 horses and 44 winches to transport the monolith on rails, using ropes. The obelisk now rests on its four corners on four cowering bronze lions (by Prospero Antiqui) on a 10-meter high base and is crowned by a cross as a sign of the victory of Christianity over paganism.

To enliven the solemnity of the huge square, made all out of stone, Maderno added in 1613, on the north side, a fountain from which transparent sheets of water would cascade down over three separate basins. In 1675 Bernini situated on the opposite side of the square a second fountain, identical with the first except that it bears the coat-of-arms of Clement X Altieri (1670-76).

From the ellipse-shaped square one passes into another, trapezoidal square closed off by two passages, 120 m long, which open out as they near the church (from 98 to 114 m) and thus make the façade seem nearer than it actually is. This was another of Bernini's ingenious solutions, to shorten the considerable distance between the obelisk and the church.

At the bottom of the wide flight of twenty two steps the two main apostles stand sentinel (since 1842). To the right is St. Paul (by Adamo Tadolini) with a sword, recalling his death by decapitation. To the left is St. Peter (by Giuseppe De Fabris) with two keys committed to him by Christ, one to "bind" and one to "loose".

On the right-hand side of the square, beyond the colonnade, is an irregular complex of buildings almost like a citadel. The first of these is the Apostolic Palace, a simple cubic-formed building in the Renaissance style, which was begun by Domenico Fontana, the architect who moved the obelisk into the square. The popes have only been living there permanently since 1870, that is, from the time that they lost the Papal States and with them the Quirinale Palace, their preferred residence. The right corner window on the top floor belongs to the pope's bedroom, while the one next to it on the left is his study window, the "window on the world". From here, every Sunday at noon, at the *Angelus*, the pope greets and blesses the crowds assembled in the piazza.

On the left of the Papal Palace is a great square courtyard, the *Cortile di San Damaso*. On the upper floor of its left-hand wing is the Secretariat of State, the highest ranking department of the Roman Curia. Further forward, to the left, is a tall building in red-brown brick with a sloping roof: inside is the Sistine Chapel, so named after Pope Sixtus IV who had it built in 1475 as his court chapel, a function it still has today. Whenever a conclave is held to elect a new pope, the Cardinals assemble in this chapel to cast their votes. The voting slips are then burned in a special stove with a high chimney emerging on the roof so that the crowd waiting in the square can tell from the color of the smoke how the voting has gone: black smoke means the majority of 75 percent plus one vote has not been obtained, while white smoke signifies that a new pontiff has been elected.

Access to the Sistine Chapel and the Apostolic Palace, for those in possession of a special pass, is by foot through the *Portone di Bronzo*, the great Bronze Gate, patrolled by the Swiss Guards in their characteristic lansquenet uniforms. Beyond the Bronze Gate one can cast a glance on the beautiful *Scala Regia*, the Royal Stairway, made by Bernini, leading up to the Royal Hall and the Sistine Chapel. On the left-hand, or southern, side of the square, one can see, through the colonnades, the yellow-brown building of the Holy Office, now called the Congregation for the Doctrine of the Faith, and the

24

24. The removal of the obelisk. This fresco, painted in 1590 by Cesare Nebbia and Giovanni Guerra in the Sala Sistina of the Vatican Library, represents the removal of the obelisk from the circus (May 7th-September 10th, 1586). In the background, on the left, are Michelangelo's transept and cupola, with work on the tambour. Between the new transept and the obelisk scaffolding is the Chapel of St. Andrew (formerly a Theodosian Rotunda), which served as the sacristy.

rounded white roof-top of the Hall of Audiences in which the pope holds his public audiences. Finished in 1971 by the architect Pier Luigi Nervi, it is the most modern structure in the Vatican. The long gallery on the left leads to the *Arco delle Campane*, the Arch of Bells, above which is the belfry, with six bells, the oldest from the 13th century and the biggest weighing 9,000 kilos.

Looking up now, we notice that St. Peter's dome has vanished from view because of the enormous height of the church's façade (114.70 × 45.50 m). Yet it is not any higher than the side walls, which already existed when Maderno lengthened the building, obliging him to build his façade to their height. The error, if any, lies in the excessive length of the central nave and in the immense size of the atrium which

25

25. Medal showing Bernini's project. This medal, made during the pontificate of Alexander VII and kept in the Vatican Library, represents the plan for St. Peter's Square, entrusted to Bernini. It had two semicircular rows of columns, and a shorter colonnade, which should have bounded the east side of the oval square, but was never erected.

alter the original organic relation between church and cupola. But, it must be said in defense of Maderno, that he had planned to build towers on both ends of the façade, thus to enshrine the cupola. Bernini had begun the tower to the left, but had to pull it down because it began to crack. To replace the towers, in 1786 Giuseppe Valadier put a huge clock on each side. And in order to elevate the façade, 13 figures (5.70 m high) were placed on top, depicting Christ, the Baptist and all the Apostles excepting Peter, who already stands at the bottom of the steps. Paul V's proud inscription extends the whole length of the façade he had built: IN. HONOREM. PRIN-CIPIS. APOST. PAULUS. V. BURGHESIUS. ROMANUS. PONT. MAX. AN. MDCXII. PONT. VII. "In honor of the Prince of the Apostles, Paul V Borghese, Roman, Supreme Pontiff, in the year 1612, the seventh year of his pontificate". In addition, he had his coat-of-arms set on top. A relief by

26. A Papal Mass. *On Church holidays, the Pope says Mass at the altar of the Confession, before the faithful who flock there from every corner of the world. Pope Wojtyla sits here in his bishop's vestments, as Bishop of Rome, while the deacons' Readings proceed, often in several languages.*

27. The Pope at the window of the Apostolic Palace. *On Sundays, the Pope goes to his studio window at twelve noon to say the* Angelus *with the faithful gathered in the square. He then makes a short, informal speech and gives them his blessing.*

28. The Pope blesses the crowd from the Loggia of Benedictions. *On the day of his election, on Christmas, on Easter, and on other important occasions, the Pope gives the solemn* urbi et orbi *blessing (to Rome and to the world) from the* Loggia *at the center of St. Peter's façade.*

29

30

29. The Bronze Doors. *This is the entrance to the Apostolic Palace. Visible in the background is Bernini's* Scala Regia, *leading to the Royal Hall and the Sistine Chapel's entrance of honor. The doors are attended by the Swiss Guard, entrusted with guarding the Pope's person and the Vatican entrances, and garbed in the same uniform worn when the corps was founded in 1506. At the end of the long corridor, where the northern colonnade begins, the Portico of Constantine lies to the right of St. Peter's churchyard.*

30. Fontain in St. Peter's Square. *On the north side of the square, level with the center of the colonnade, the great fountain built by Carlo Maderno in 1613 shoots wide streams of water into three superposed basins, inspiring these famous lines of the Swiss poet, Conrad Ferdinand Meyer (1882): "... and each gives and takes at once / and flows and rests."*.

Ambrogio Buonvicino (about 1614) over the main entrance represents the Entrusting of the Keys.

The attentive observer may notice that the center of the façade does not exactly align with the center of the dome. Maderno had to swing slightly the longhouse of the church and consequently the façade to the left, that is to the south, in order to get the center of the façade in line with the obelisk of the square in front of it. The obelisk, being erected before the dome was finished, is not quite on the same axis as the dome.

The central point of the façade is the famous *Loggia*. From here the pope imparts his solemn blessing *urbi et orbi* (to the city and to the whole world) on solemn occasions. From here the cardinal deacon announces the name of the newly elected pope. For a canonization or beatification, a tapestry with the image of the new saint or blessed is uncovered from the *Loggia*.

31

32

The Atrium of St. Peter's

31. 32.   Charlemagne and Constantine. The statues of the Christian Emperors bound up with the church's history embody the idea of the Empire, "secular arm" of the Church. The former is by Cornacchini (1725), the latter by Bernini (1670).

The atrium or portico of the basilica is as large as a church (71 × 13 × 20 m). On its floor is inlaid the coat-of-arms of Pope John XXIII Roncalli (1958-63), in polychrome marble, to commemorate the opening of Vatican Council II which he convened in 1962. The ceiling is richly decorated in gilt stucco-work. There are five big bronze doors to the basilica. The main one is only opened on special occasions. It has survived the demolition of the old basilica and was made during the years 1440-45 by Antonio di Pietro Averulino (known as il Filarete), for Eugene IV Condulmer (1431-47). It was the first work of Renaissance art to be done in Rome, although by a Florentine artist. The new spirit of the Renaissance manifests itself by the representations of contemporary political events, such as the incoronation of the Emperor Sigismund in Rome in 1433 and the Council of Ferrara-Florence in 1438-45, and by the interest shown in pagan antiquity (heads of Roman emperors and mythological scenes in the framework).

The next door to the right is by Venanzio Crocetti (1964) and shows the seven Sacraments. This is the usual entrance for visitors.

The far door to the right is the Holy Door. The pope himself opens it by knocking at it three times with a silver hammer, on Christmas Eve, to mark the beginning of a Holy Year. At the end of the year, the pope closes the door again with solemnity, after which it remains walled up for 24 years. This custom, introduced by Alexander VI Borgia (1492-1503) on Christmas Eve 1499, expresses the admission to grace, to eternal life, to Christ himself, who had said "I am the Door" (John 10, 9). The bronze door wings are modern, made by Vico Consorti in 1950, and represent biblical episodes referring to the aim of all Holy Years: the reconciliation between men and God. Up on the wall to the left of the Holy Door

33

33. The Portico. *It was built between 1608 and 1612 by Carlo Maderno. His nephew, Francesco Borromini, whose only work in the basilica is the magnificent gate to the Chapel of the Blessed Sacrament, was a mere "chisel-cutter" on the stuccoes, designed by Maderno himself. The five openings on the right correspond to the five bronze entrance doors to St. Peter's. They are all modern, excepting the Main Gate, which was made during the Renaissance and comes from the old basilica.*

34

35

is a marble plate with the text of the bull of Boniface VIII Caetani (1294-1303), proclaiming the first Jubilee Year in 1300. He intended it to be repeated every 100 years in memory of the birth of Christ. So far there have been 25 Holy Years, as they have been celebrated every 25 years since 1555.

Two further tablets between the doors are an act of donation by Gregory II (715-31) of olive-groves to provide the oil for the lamps round the tomb of Peter and a funeral elegy dedicated by Charlemagne (742-814) to his "friend and father" Pope Hadrian I (772-795).

On the far left is the Door of Death (1964) by Giacomo Manzù, so-called because it bears representations of the many ways in which man may die. Above, victory over the death of the body is symbolized by the Assumption of Mary into heaven. The artist also sculpted John XXIII kneeling, as it was he who convinced him after years of uncertainty to complete the work so that the patrimony of Prince George of Bavaria (d. 1942), canon of St. Peter's, which he had bequeathed in his will for this purpose, would not be invalidated by prescription.

The most recent door is the second one from the left,

by Luciano Minguzzi, added in 1977. Its theme is "Good and Evil".

At the outer ends of the entrance hall are two equestrian statues. To the right stands Emperor Constantine by Gian Lorenzo Bernini (1670) and, opposite, Charlemagne by Agostino Cornacchini (1725). The two statues were placed here to demonstrate that the Christian emperors were once considered the secular protectors and defenders of the Church.

If we then turn around, we can see, high above the main gate, a mosaic, originally placed in the atrium of the old basilica and probably designed by Giotto in 1298 on a commission from Cardinal Stefaneschi, who kneels as donor in the low right corner. It is called *La Navicella* (the small ship) because it depicts Peter's fishing boat in the squall on Lake Genesareth. Peter, eager to hurry across the water to Christ, is on the point of drowning. Christ then holds out a hand to him and pulls him to safety (Matthew 14, 26-33). This is in fact the underlying theme of St. Peter's church: it will stand, because Christ is its support. Only in the knowledge of this, can we enter, and understand, St. Peter's church.

34. The Main Gate to St. Peter's. *This detail of the door's right wing shows St. Peter with Pope Eugene IV, who commissioned the door from Antonio Averulino, called "Il Filarete", to commemorate the Ecumenical Council of Florence (1438-45), which ratified — though only for a short while — the union of the Eastern and Western Churches.*

35. The Door of Death, detail of right wing. *Inaugurated in 1964, this door was made by Giacomo Manzù for Pope John XXIII, who is shown kneeling here in profile.*

36. The Porta Santa with Paul VI. *This door was last opend and closed for the Holy Year 1975, proclaimed by Paul VI. Its friezes show the coats of arms of the 27 popes who celebrated a Holy Year after 1300.*

37. The "Navicella". *Although this mosaic has been altered by retouching, Giotto's pictorial language still transpires. In 1298 he was commissioned by Cardinal Jacopo Stefaneschi to prepare it for the Jubilee of 1300. It decorated the interior of the Constantinian atrium, facing the façade. Its present position dates from 1675.*

36

37

38

The Interior of St. Peter's

38.   The Naves. *Built by Maderno (1607-14) and later decorated by baroque artists. The polychrome floor with its parallel lines helps create a dynamic perspective, guiding the steps of the faithful towards the heart of the church, the* Confessio.

We enter now through the Door of the Seven Sacraments and, whether pilgrim or tourist, believer or non-believer, we cannot but be overwhelmed on first glimpsing the brightness, vastness and majesty of this splendid "throne hall". For this was precisely the intention of Bernini when he created the decoration of the church: to convey a glance of the heavenly throne and glory of God. One could say that St. Peter's has three aspects: it was founded as *Memoria Petri* (memorial of Peter), it became the coronation hall for popes and emperors, and it is always and foremost the house of God, where the faithful from all over the world for almost 2,000 years have come to praise Him.

In order to seize at a glance the form and spirit of the church, we should first of all step to the rear of the main door and place ourselves right in the center. From here it is possible to see the whole length of the central nave as far as the papal altar with the light

falling on it from the cupola high above and, further on still, through the altar canopy to the gilded throne, the *Cathedra Petri*, visible under the far vault of the apse. In the window of Bohemian crystal immediately above is a dove with outstretched wings, surrounded with golden beams, as though giving visible proof of Christ's words that the Holy Spirit animates the Church of God.

At the spot where we stand, there is an inscription in bronze lettering on the floor to the effect that the Vatican temple is 186.36 m long, and including the walls (but without the atrium) 192.76 m. It is thus the longest church in the world. In evidence of this, the dimensions of other big churches are inscribed on the floor of the central nave. The second longest is St. Paul's Cathedral in London, though, as a mark of respect, ten meters shorter. The floor of polychrome marble slabs forms a geometric design on a white ground. Next to the entrance is a round

39.   Michelangelo's Pietà. *This is the first of four variations on the same theme sculpted by Michelangelo during his long lifetime. The perfect union of Mother and Son in grief and sacrifice is beautifully expressed in the circular fluidity of an ideal line which runs from the reclining head of the Madonna along her right arm to the limp head of Christ, and from there follows the hem of her dress parallel to the Son's lifeless arm, finally returning upwards to her left hand and, at last, to her face.*

disc of red porphyry, called *rota*. This precious mineral indicates already that the slab has a special significance, because porphyry, like purple, was once used only for holy places and high dignitaries. It comes from the old basilica and was the area reserved for the judges of the Sacred Rota, who did in fact hold their meetings on it, and for emperors when they took part in religious functions in St. Peter's.

It is said that Charlemagne knelt there for his coronation as Roman emperor on Christmas day in the year 800, and another 22 emperors after him. The last to be crowned here was Frederick III of Hapsburg who received the imperial crown in 1452 from Nicholas V.

New St. Peter's has, as is known, a Latin-cross ground plan, that is a longstretched long nave and a short cross nave with a dome in the point of intersection. Old St. Peter's was in the style of a basilica with five equal long naves. New St. Peter's has only three naves but with three chapels on both sides. The new church is not, as the previous one was, roofed by a wooden ceiling resting on columns, but by a barrel vault ceiling supported by pilasters; instead of the old twilight atmosphere, now the bright sunlight floods it. With this, New St. Peter's came to be the model for all the other churches built during the Counter-Reformation. Whereas the first basilica was in red brick, the second is in white travertine in the Renaissance style. On the inside the walls are not covered with frescoes but with marble, mosaics and stucco-work, of which the tones range from golden-yellow to reddish-brown. The whole of the interior decoration was conceived by Bernini and his assistants in the spirit of the Baroque, which aimed at merging marble and mosaics, gold and stucco, sculpture and architecture, in short, all the elements, colors and forms, in a strikingly harmonious way.

On the first pilasters on both sides of the middle nave are two gigantic holy water stoups supported by chubby putti in white marble. The third pilaster on each side stands a meter further forward into the nave and marks how far Michelangelo's work had reached. Maderno reduced the circumference of his own pilasters, the first two on either side seen from the entrance, thus increasing the area of the central nave as compared with that of the old basilica, from 25.84 m to 28.90 m. He also raised the ceiling slightly, and built in three windows on each side, which made his building clearer and lighter. Apart from these details, Maderno's addition blends in perfectly with Michelangelo's creation.

On the outer faces of the pilasters are satues of the founders of religious orders, 39 in all, while on the inner faces are medallions, held up by putti, of the first 56 holy popes. In between we find the motif of a dove with an olive branch in its beak: it is the emblem of Innocent X Pamphilj (1644-55) in whose pontificate the pilasters were decorated.

Above the pilasters is an inscription (593 m long and 2 m high) in black letters on gold ground, with quotations from Holy Scripture referring to Peter's mandate, in both Latin and Greek, to emphasize the Church's universality. Above that is the barrel vault ceiling (44.50 m high, 27 m wide) decorated with gilded coffers and rosettes.

Besides the big central cupola, there are ten smaller ones: four of them are round and were designed by Michelangelo, situated over the corner chapels; and six are oval, put up by Maderno over the two side naves. They are all worked in mosaics, because mosaic deteriorates much less than a painting would. A special workshop, the *Studio del Mosaico*, was founded in 1727 to decorate St. Peter's, and still exists in the Vatican, restoring old mosaics and manufacturing new ones.

A visit to St. Peter's usually starts from the first side-chapel on the right. Here we see at once the greatest art treasure of St. Peter's: Michelangelo's *Pietà*. The "*Pietà*", or representation of the Blessed Mother weeping over the dead body of her Son in her lap, was a popular theme in mediaeval art and corresponded to the deeply religious and melancholic nature of Michelangelo, who all his life long meditated on this theme and created as many as four statues of the Pietà. Yet the most beautiful one and the only one completed is this one, the first, which he started to work on in 1498, at the age of 23, for the chapel of St. Petronilla, which was placed under the patronage of the kings of France. The work stayed there until the chapel was destroyed in 1544, and found its present site in 1749. A bulletproof glass wall was recently placed in front of it, after a deranged individual tried to demolish the statue with a hammer in 1972. That is why we cannot get close enough to see the beautiful face of Christ nor read Michelangelo's signature on the ribbon crossing the shoulder of Mary. It is in fact the only work to have been signed by Michelangelo, some time after he had finished it. Having overheard a discussion between two men from Lombardy attributing it to a mediocre artist of their home town, Michelangelo was so annoyed that he went back into the church during the night and chiseled into the ribbon of Mary: MICHAEL. ĀGELUS. BONAROTUS. FLORENT. FACIEBAT.

The statue is made of one single block of candid Car-

40

41

40.   Monument of Christina of Sweden. *In this monument, designed by Carlo Fontana in about 1700, the medallion and the sarcophagus relief are by J.-Baptiste Théodon. Innocent XII commissioned the monument in honor of Christina's sacrifice of her throne to join the Roman Church, and perhaps because he wished to use her example to encourage Sweden to return to Catholicism.*

41.   Monument of Matilda of Canossa. *Designed by Gian Lorenzo Bernini and executed by his brother, Luigi, and his pupil, Andrea Bolgi, this piece was inaugurated in 1637. The sarcophagus is by Stefano Speranza. The epitaph dedication is "virilis animi foeminae", "to the woman of virile soul".*

42.   Monument to Pius XII. *This bronze statue (1964) was commissioned from Francesco Messina by the cardinals appointed by Pius XII.*

42

43

44

rara marble, as if to show the complete unity between mother and son. The much-too-young face of the Blessed Virgin is meant by Michelangelo to manifest her perfect purity of mind and body and expresses a tender resignation, as if she wanted to say once more as she did to the angel of the Annunciation: "Let what you have said be done unto me" (Luke 1, 38). Also the dead body of Christ seems so beautiful and vivid, as if he were to resurrect at any moment. A great consolation seems to emanate from this sublime work of art.

Besides the 147 popes, there are also six women buried in St. Peter's whose tombs still exist (there were more, but in the course of time these have been destroyed). The first we encounter in front of the *Pietà*: she is Queen Christina of Sweden (1626-89), who had inherited the throne while still a child after her father, Gustav Adolph, fell in the Thirty Years War as defender of Lutheranism. She was an exceptionally gifted woman, with a craving for learning. At the age of 28 she decided to become a Catholic. Therefore, she had to renounce her throne and leave her country. She formally abjured the Protestant faith in the Court church of Innsbruck in 1655. This scene is represented on the outer side of the sar-

43.   Tabernacle of the Chapel of the Blessed Sacrament. *For this late work (1675), Bernini took as his model Bramante's* Tempietto *for the* S. Pietro in Montorio *courtyard, inspired by the round temples of the Roman Vestal Virgins. Just as there sacred fire, symbol of eternal Rome, was kept, here lay the consecrated Hosts, pledge of Eternal Life in Christ.*

44.   Bronze statue of St. Peter, *done shortly before 1300 and attributed to Arnolfo di Cambio. Peter holds the two symbolic keys to the kingdom of Heaven and blesses in Greek fashion, his index and middle finger raised to indicate the two-fold nature of Christ, the others pressed together in the sign of the Trinity.*

45.   St. Peter with sacred vestments. *On St. Peter's day (June 29th) the statue is dressed as a Pope on the throne, with tiara, brocade mantle with precious clasp, and Fisherman's Ring.*

46.   Statue of Veronica. *In this colossal statue sculpted in 1646 by Francesco Mochi, an extreme example of high Baroque taste for the expression of passions exaggerated nearly to the point of artifice.*

45

46

cophagus. Once in Rome, Christina became the central figure of the social and cultural life of the city. Because she had sacrificed her throne for her faith, she was buried with royal honors in St. Peter's. Carlo Fontana erected this monument to her in 1700. Her mortal remains lie in a simple stone sarcophagus in the Grottoes. By a strange quirk of fate, the pope with whom Queen Christina had frequently been at loggerheads as a result of her lavish and extravagant life-style is at rest directly opposite her, mummified in a crystal urn, through which he must look at her even in death. This is Innocent XI Odescalchi (1676-89), who was beatified in 1958.

Above the altar of Innocent XI is the mosaic copy of a big painting by Domenichino depicting the Martyrdom of St. Sebastian (1629). The original is in St. Mary of the Angels.

To the right of the altar is the seated figure of Pius XI Ratti (1922-39), a work of Francesco Nagni (1964). Opposite it is the statue of Pius XII Pacelli (1939-58), wrapped in a heavy brocade cloak of bronze, his forehead deeply furrowed and his hand lifted in a self-protective gesture as if to ward off the horrors of war and dictatorship which he foresees as the lot of his pontificate. The aristocratic and almost

stately detachment of Pius XII is magnificently expressed in this work of Francesco Messina (1964).

Another tomb of a woman, by the next pilaster on the left, belongs to Matilda of Tuscany (1046-1115), the most powerful woman of her time. She controlled the whole of Northern Italy and all roads to Rome from her ancestral castle at Canossa. The statue holds the sceptre in its right hand, while in the left it carries the keys of Peter and even the papal tiara. Bernini, who created the monument in 1635, meant by this to bear witness to the fact that Matilda was the greatest ally of the papacy in the fight for Church reform and freedom against the German King Henry IV, a monarch anxious to take over the episcopal investitures for himself. On the bas-relief of the sarcophagus (by Stefano Speranza, 1635) we see the famous scene which took place in Canossa in January 1077, in which the excommunicated Henry IV, dressed as a penitent, makes the act of submission to the Pope, while Matilda points to him in a gesture of mediation. She died without heirs and left all her possessions to the Roman Church. The bones of Matilda were removed to Rome 500 years after her death, when Urban VIII wanted to enrich the new church of St. Peter's with the tombs of famous per-

47

sonalities and defenders of the papacy.

Opposite Matilda's monument is the one to Innocent XII Pignatelli (1691-1700). On his left is the Chapel of the Blessed Sacrament, for which Bernini designed the tabernacle in the form of a circular shrine, in gilt bronze and lapis-lazuli. This tabernacle recalls Bramante's "*tempietto*" in San Pietro in Montorio and, going back even further in time, the Roman temples of Vesta, which also were round and enclosed by columns. There the Vestal Virgins guarded the sacred fire, symbol of the eternal life of Rome; here in the tabernacle the consecrated hosts are kept, the tokens of eternal life in Christ. Two magnificent angels, also in gilt bronze, frame the tabernacle with their wings. The altarpiece, by Pietro da Cortona, depicts the Trinity and is the only oil painting left in St. Peter's.

The monument to Gregory XIII Boncompagni (1572-85) comes next. This pope was a great promoter of natural sciences. He founded the Vatican Astronomical Observatory and introduced the reform of the calendar, called after him the Gregorian Calendar and still in use. This papal act, to which all nations eventually adhered, is

47.   The Niche of the Pallia. *It is in the crypt, with decoration by Carlo Maderno (1600). In the Middle Ages, bandages lowered from a tombstone at its base to touch Peter's grave were afterwards considered religious relics "by contact".*

48.   The Papal Altar. *Bernini's monumental canopy exhalts the papal altar without obstructing the structures around it. The effect of its height is to shorten the distance from the cupola, and to produce an optical reduction of the lenght of the nave.*

represented on the relief of the tomb by Carlo Melloni (1723).

The right-hand side nave, down which we have been walking, ends in front of the mosaic of St. Jerome, who receives his last communion from St. Ephraim at Bethlehem while his favorite disciple, St. Paula, kisses his hands in farewell. It is a reproduction from a masterpiece by Domenichino (1614) in which the weak, consumptive body of the dying Jerome is wonderfully captured. (The original is in the Vatican Pinacotheca).

49

49. Vatican Council II took place between 1962 and 1965, in four sessions. Special stalls were set up in the central nave to hold the nearly 3,000 bishops attending, whereas for Vatican Council I (1869-70) the transept right wing had been sufficient. Observers from non-Catholic churches were seated up front, on the right, and the papal throne was placed above the Confession.

50. Interior of the Cupola. Michelangelo did not live to see his cupola, for it was finished during the Pontificate of Sixtus V, 26 years after his death. Its mosaics, made at the end of the 16th century mainly from cartoons by Cavalier d'Arpino (Giuseppe Cesari), are among the most valuable ones in the basilica and, unlike the altar-piece mosaics, were composed especially for it, as were those in the smaller cupolas of the transept.

Here starts Michelangelo's huge ambulatory around the outside of the pilasters supporting the cupola. This passageway forms a square with a large chapel in each of the four corners. The first, to our right, is called the Gregorian Chapel, after Gregory 12th, in whose pontificate Giacomo Della Porta in 1583 completed work on it and decorated it lavishly in marble and mosaics. In the altar is kept the urn containing the mortal remains of the Greek Father of the Church, St. Gregory of Nazianzus, Patriarch of Constantinople (330-390). Above the altar is the image of the Madonna of Succour, a 12th century work, moved here from the old basilica.

We now turn left from the altar of St. Jerome into the main aisle. Here, under the north-eastern pilaster, we find the famous bronze statue of Peter, sitting on his throne with a severe look, one hand holding fast to his keys, the other blessing in the Greek way. His extended right foot has become shiny and worn from the kisses of the faithful. The statue is considered to be a work of Arnolfo di Cambio, who was active in Rome around the year 1300. High above the statue a portrait in mosaic of Pius IX Mastai-Ferretti (1846-78) can be seen. He had it placed there himself when, in 1871, he reached the «years of Peter», i.e. 25 years of Pontificate (it being believed that Peter was bishop of Rome from 42 to 67).

Now we enter the bright light that falls in great shafts from the cupola above onto the Confession. The Latin word *"confessio"* refers to the tomb of a martyr. It also stands for the place where the faithful come to profess the same faith for which the martyr

died. Here ''confession'' means the very tomb of Peter. Two marble staircases lead to a semi-circular open crypt, built by Maderno around 1600. Down below, a gilded gate opens into a niche with a Byzantine mosaic of Christ the Savior in the background. It is called the ''Niche of the Sacred Pallia'' because it contains in the center a golden eighteenth-century box where the *pallia* are kept: these are narrow white stoles which the Pope bestows on every new Metropolitan, and until that time they are kept here at the tomb of Peter as a symbol of the close link between Rome and the local churches. The niche is enshrined by three marble slabs, one to the left and two to the right. Here we notice an odd lack of symmetry, because the Niche of the Pallia is not directly in line with the center of the gateway, and the longitudinal axis of the church does not exactly run through it but slightly to the right towards North, as if the builders of the church were somehow aware of the importance of the right side of the Niche. Behind it, in fact, is the famous ''Wall g'' in which the bones of Peter have been concealed since the time of Constantine.

On the other side of the papal altar, set into the floor, there is a round grating through which we can see down into the heart of St. Peter's church, into the Chapel of Peter which adjoins the tomb of the Apostle at the back. The whole church is in effect a vast and priceless reliquary built over and around this tomb. Here, we stand at the focal point of the church and, at the same time, at the intersection of two lines which cross the building: the horizontal line starts at the obelisk outside and leads across the

50

Confession to the *Cathedra Petri* in the apse; the vertical line starts in the depths of Peter's tomb and leads across the Papal Altar to the summit of the cupola. These two lines make up a cross, and the cross is the essence of Christian life.

Above the sepulchre of the Apostle is the Papal Altar itself, made from a big block of white marble taken from the Forum of Nerva and consecrated by Clement VIII Aldobrandini (1592-1605) in 1594. The altar, facing the congregation, looks eastward to the rising sun, as was the custom whenever possible in early Christian churches. Above the altar and supported by four gigantic twisted bronze columns, which shorten optically the enormous distance between the ground floor and the dome, is a canopy of gilded bronze which not only enshrines the altar and the tomb below, but also serves as a stately frame for the *Cathedra Petri*, at the rear of the apse. It is Bernini's masterpiece: he worked on it for ten years and completed it in 1633. It marks the triumph of the Baroque style over the plain lines of the Renaissance in which the church was built. The twisted bronze columns remind us of the ancient marble columns which stood round the tomb of Peter in the Constan-

tine basilica; these were decorated with vine-shoots, whereas the Baroque columns are worked in olive leaves. Swarms of bronze bees, the heraldic emblem of the Barberini princes, can be seen all round the canopy. It was in fact commissioned by a Barberini pope, Urban VIII. Given the scarcity of bronze at that time, Urban ordered Bernini to remove the bronze beams from the Pantheon and use that material. Not even the barbarians had perpetrated such an act; hence the Romans coined the epigram: *Quod non fecerunt barbari, fecerunt Barberini* (what the barbarians did not do, the Barberini did).

Above the canopy we look into the cupola, the last and greatest work by Michelangelo. The cupola bends down upon us as the paternal hands of God the Father, protecting precisely the tomb of the First Vicar of Christ.

The dome rests on four grandiose pentagonal pilasters with a perimeter of 71 m. They are 25 m high, and the summit of the connecting arches reaches the height of 44.37 m. In the niches of the four pilasters stand the imposing marble figures of four saints who carry the emblem of a relic conserved and venerated in St. Peter's: St. Longinus (by Bernini, 1639) with the lance which pierced Christ's side; St. Helena, with the actual Cross she found, a fragment of which she brought to Rome (by Andrea Bolgi, 1639); St. Andrew, younger brother of Peter, carrying an oblique cross on which he was crucified (by Frans Duquesnoy, 1640); and St. Veronica (by Francesco Mochi, 1639), hurrying, amazed, to display the veil on which Christ had left the impression of his features.

Three transept areas of equal length radiate out from the Confession, symbolizing the Trinity. We first enter the right-hand or northern transept. There the First Vatican Council of 1869-70, with an assembly of 700 bishops, took place. But a century later it could not contain the 3,000 bishops attending Vatican Council II (1962-65), with the result that long tribunes had to be built up on both sides of the central nave.

In the apse of this transept (45 m long) is the altar of the martyrs Processus and Martinianus, framed by two precious porphyry columns from the older tabernacle built by Sixtus IV above the papal altar. The subject of the mosaic above it is the martyrdom of St. Peter's two jailers whom, according to tradition, he converted and baptized. To the left is a mosaic from a picture by Nicolas Poussin (about 1630): it is the Martyrdom of St. Erasmus, bishop of Formia (the original is in the Vatican Pinacotheca).

To the right, in the passageway to the Gregorian Chapel, is an altar dedicated to the Christian Orient. The altarpiece represents St. Basil the Great as he converts the Aryan Emperor Valens in 732. Set into the altar itself is a crystal urn containing the body of St. Josaphat, clad in Byzantine vestments. He was the Ukrainian archbishop of Kiev, killed in 1623 by the Russian Orthodox because of his loyalty to Rome.

Further on, to the left, in the corridor leading to the Chapel of St. Petronilla, is an altarpiece in mosaic, after a painting by Giovanni Lanfranco (1628) representing the *Navicella*, the fundamental theme of the church.

Opposite is the tomb of Clement XIII Rezzonico (1758-69), a masterpiece by Antonio Canova with which in 1797 the severe "white" Neo-classical style entered St. Peter's in reaction to the exuberance of the Baroque. Two magnificent lions, one sleeping and one alert, guard the entrance to the tomb, and behind them stand the allegorical figures of Religion and the Genius of Death. It is said that when the tomb was consecrated, Canova mingled with the crowd to hear what they thought about his work. But

51

51. The Wooden Throne. *This oaken chair decorated in gold and ivory, the alleged throne of Peter, was built for Charles the Bald (he may be the monarch portrayed at the center of the back) who donated it to the Pope for his imperial coronation (875). In the facsimile on display in the Treasury Museum, the ancient panel arrangement, altered during the Middle Ages, has been restored.*

52. The Throne of St. Peter in Glory. *Gigantic, ornate reliquary done (1658-66) by Bernini to enclose the crumbling "Throne of Peter". The bronze chair seems suspended on high with a wonderfully light effect.*

as he had disguised himself as a beggar to avoid recognition, Prince Rezzonico gave him alms and insisted he leave the premises.

We come now to the Chapel of St. Petronilla itself. It was in the Catacombs of Domitilla that a sarcophagus was discovered in the eighth century of a "dearest daughter Petronilla", as the inscription reads. People at that time thought that the name Petronilla was a derivation from Petrus and so a legend grew up that she had been the Apostle Peter's young daughter and had died a martyr. Her

54

55

53

53. Tomb of Paul III. *On this monument by Guglielmo della Porta (1576) allegorical female figures appear on a papal tomb for the first time.*

54. Tomb of Urban VIII. *In this work of Bernini's, high Baroque redundancy triumphs.*

55. Tomb of Alexander VII. *Designed by Bernini, nearly 80, who also sculpted the Pope's head. In the foreground, Charity and Truth (who tramples on the terrestrial sphere).*

56. Tomb of Leo XI. *In this sober white monument, Alessandro Algardi rejects Bernini's reigning Baroque style. The figures of Courage and Generosity are by Ercole Ferrata and Giuseppe Peroni, two worthy representatives of mid-17th century art.*

57. Tomb of Clement XIII. *This work by Antonio Canova (1797), is the first example of Neoclassicism in St. Peter's.*

58. Tomb of Pius VII. *Thorvaldsen, a pupil of Canova, dedicated one of his most academic works to the humble, generous Pope, persecuted by Napoleon.*

56

57

bones were duly moved, to be near the remains of her supposed father in an antique mausoleum to the left of the ancient basilica, which was accordingly named *la Rotonda di S. Petronilla*. Later on it was also called the "Chapel of the Kings of France" because Petronilla had come to be venerated as the French patron saint. When the rotunda had to give way to the new church, the relics of Petronilla were placed in this altar, for which Guercino did a much-admired altarpiece (1623) representing the burial and glorification into heaven of this young and beautiful saint. The painting, now in the Capitoline Museum, is replaced here with a copy in mosaic by Pietro Paolo Cristofari, the first director of the Vatican mosaics workshop.

Under the floor of this chapel are buried some members of the della Rovere family, among them the Popes Sixtus IV and Julius II. It was Julius II who had laid the foundation stone of the new church, in which his own magnificent mausoleum was supposed to have had a place of honor. Instead he is now at rest here in plain earth, without any tombstone. His funeral monument, which he had commissioned from Michelangelo during his lifetime, was never finished. Only part of it, with the famous statue of

58

Moses, survives today in another church dedicated to the Apostle, that of San Pietro in Vincoli.

Between the tomb of Clement X, with a marble relief by Leonardo Leli depicting the Pope in the act of opening the Holy Door (1675) and the St. Petronilla altar, a door in the wall leads to the Archives of the *Reverenda Fabbrica di S. Pietro*, the administration office of St. Peter's, situated in the interspace of the cupola. The church's thick walls contain a labyrinth of corridors, spiral staircases and recesses through which only the *sampietrini*, the workmen of St. Peter's, know their way. They have formed a special guild of about 100 men during the last 400 years.

Finally we enter the apse, where two wide steps of porphyry, originally from the old basilica, now lead to the *Cathedra Petri*. This is the terminal point of a spiritual procession starting at the obelisk in the square, moving through the great atrium, down the long central nave, passing the Confession and finally reaching the *Cathedra*, the symbolic chair of Peter. The casing of gold and bronze is a protective cover, like a huge reliquary. It contains a wooden chair, once believed to be the chair of the Apostle. In reality it was a throne which the Emperor Charles the Bald (823-877) brought with him for his coronation in 875 and then donated to the Pope. When the wooden throne became unusable because of its age, Bernini (1666) enclosed it in a new throne of bronze and raised it above the altar in a setting of clouds, light rays and angels. Below it are the statues of four Fathers of the Church: two from the West, wearing mitres, Ambrose and Augustine; and two from the East, Athanasius and John Chrysostom, (without the mitres, not worn in the Eastern Church). The four Church Fathers are not actually carrying the throne, but merely touch it, as if to say that the pope rules over the universal Church with the bishops, and the bishops rule with him, neither without the other. With this Bernini has already, knowingly or unknowingly, expressed the idea of the collegiality of the bishops with the pope, an idea enunciated only at the last Vatican Council.

Still in another regard Bernini anticipated his time: he represented the idea of the infallibility of the Pope 200 years before it was proclaimed a dogma, in 1870. He did this by means of the dove with open wings in the center of the window above the *Cathedra*, as if to say that the Holy Ghost illuminates the pope when he speaks *ex cathedra*, from the throne, and defines a dogma. In this bold and genial work, Baroque art achieves its apogee. All the ingredients are there: architecture and sculpture, gold and glass, marble and bronze, light and shadow, in order to give visible form and honor to the doctrine of the infallibility of the Pontiff.

On the left, near the throne, is the monument to Paul III. The pontiff is at rest in an antique sarcophagus of precious black marble. At its feet are sitting two allegorical female figures, a feature which from that time on became common for papal tombs. The woman on the left represents Justice: originally this figure was a nude, but then it was chastely covered in a penitential tunic of metal. The other figure is a melancholy old woman personifying Wisdom, a virtue not attained until old age, when external attractiveness is no more: hence the figure is left nude. The monument was built by Guglielmo Della Porta with the help of Michelangelo (1551-75). On the right-hand side of the throne is the tomb of Urban VIII, the great patron of Bernini, who put up this monument to express his gratitude. It subsequently became the model for all Baroque funeral monuments. Here, for the first time in funeral art appears the winged skeleton, which cancels the name of the deceased. And the Barberini family bees, seen a short while ago cheerfully buzzing about the canopy of the papal altar, now alight, confused and weary, on the tomb.

From the apse we now go left, round the two southern pilasters of the cupola. Here, on the right-hand side, is the tomb of Alexander VIII Ottoboni (1689-91) which is remarkable only for the value of its materials (onyx and polychrome marble). Then comes the Chapel of the Column, a name alluding to the ancient fresco of the Madonna painted on a column which was moved here from the ancient basilica. In the altar itself are the mortal remains of three holy popes: Leo II (682-683), Leo III (795-816) and Leo IV (847-855). On the right is the altar of Saint Leo I the Great (440-461), who saved Rome from conquest and pillage by the Huns. The historic meeting (452) between the Pope and Attila, King of the Huns, is represented here in a masterly marble relief by Alessandro Algardi (1650).

Above the door, which leads from the church into Piazza di S. Marta inside the Vatican City, is the tomb of Alexander VII. During this pope's reign, the Baroque reached its full maturity. It was on Alexander's commission that Bernini created St. Peter's Square, and to him he dedicated his last work, which already announces the dissolution of the Baroque. Again the winged skeleton of Death is featured, as on the tomb of Urban VIII, appearing from behind a heavy curtain of Sicilian jasper, and upturning an hour-glass to show that the pope's time has run its

59

60

59. The Transfiguration. *A masterful 18th-century mosaic copy of Raphael's last work (1520), by the Vatican Mosaic Studio. Although attempts to substitute paintings with mosaics in St. Peter's date from the 17th century, or even earlier, the Studio was officially founded in 1727.*

60. The Choir Chapel. *This ornate chapel was decorated during the first half of the 17th century. Bernini designed the wooden stalls and G. Battista Ricci did the gilded stuccoes.*

course. As usual, there are two female figures at the foot of the monument: Charity and Truth, behind which one can see the heads of Wisdom and Justice. As has the figure of Justice on the tomb of Paul II, the nude Truth here has been covered, because when he inaugurated the monument, Innocent XI commented: "Not everyone can bear the naked truth, but this one could be too pleasing to many observers".

We now come to the left-hand, or southern, transept, built by Michelangelo himself, and model for the northern one. In the apse there are three altars: the central one contains the bones of the Apostles Simon and Judas Thaddeus, whose help is invoked especially for desperate cases. To the left, above the altar, is a copy in mosaic of the painting (about 1600) by Guido Reni (now in the Vatican Pinacotheca) depicting the Crucifixion of Peter with his head downwards.

In the next corridor is the last altarpiece dedicated to the life of Peter. It is by Pomarancio (1607), and shows the episode in which Ananias and his wife Sapphira, who had lied to Peter, fall dead at the Apostle's feet (*Acts* 5, 1-11). Opposite, a passageway leads into the Sacristy and the Museum of St. Peter's. Above the door is the monument of Pius VIII Castiglioni (1829-30). But of much greater interest is the next tomb, of Pius VII Chiaramonti (1800-23), created by the Danish sculptor Bertel Thorvaldsen, a pupil of Canova, and the only Protestant artist to work in St. Peter's. It is a pyramid in white marble, typical of Neo-classical taste, and appears cold and academic.

We are now in the Clementine Chapel, begun by Michelangelo. It gets its name from Clement VIII Aldobrandini (1592-1605), during whose reign it was completed by Giacomo Della Porta. To the right of the monument to Pius VII is the altar of St.

Gregory I the Great (590-604): this great Roman (595-604) made of Rome a new starting point of conquest, this time a peaceful one, by sending out his missionaries to convert England.

In the Clementine Chapel there is also a mosaic copy of Raphael's last work, The Transfiguration of Christ on Mount Tabor. Raphael died while he was still at work on this in 1520. The painting was put up at the foot of his bier, ''causing any man who looked at it to feel that his heart must burst with grief'', as Vasari reports. The original, once in S. Pietro in Montorio, then purloined by Napoleon and taken to Paris, is now permanently in the Vatican Pinacotheca.

And so we head towards the exit through the left-hand (or southern) side-nave, where we find two facing monuments: on the left, the one belonging to Innocent XI, with a relief portraying the deliverance of Vienna from the Turks in 1683, the most important event in his pontificate, which put an end to the Islamic threat to European Christianity.

Opposite lies the fourth and last Medici pope, Leo XI, who reigned for only 27 days in 1606: hence the

61.   Monument to Innocent VIII. *This tomb by Antonio del Pollaiolo (1498) is the only one from the old basilica to be put back up in the new one. In the panels are the cardinal virtues, Fortitude, Justice, Temperance, Prudence, and, above, the theological virtues with the supreme virtue, Charity, between Faith and winged Hope.*

62.   Monument to John XXIII. *Bronze relief by Emilio Greco (1970).*

63.   Monument of Mary Clementine Stuart Sobiesky. *The figure of Charity raising the pious sovereign's inflamed heart was done in 1745 by Filippo Barigioni, a late imitator of Bernini. The graceful mosaic portrait is by Pietro Paolo Cristofari, first Superintendent of the Mosaic Studio.*

64.   Monument of the last Stuarts. *The neoclassical stele by Antonio Canova (1819), justly famed for its pure beauty, is perhaps the most linear monument in the basilica. The two mourning winged figures are reminiscent of ancient Greek ephebes.*

63

64

withered roses reproduced on the pedestal of the monument with the motto SIC FLORUI ("Thus I bloomed"). The tomb is by Algardi, who did not share the penchant for the Baroque excess of his great rival Bernini. In the relief are two scenes from the life of the deceased when he was still pontifical legate in France and in that capacity had received Henry IV's abjuration from Protestantism (1593).

To the left is the Chapel of the Choir, parallel to the Chapel of the Blessed Sacrament, where the canons of St. Peter's assemble to recite the Daily Office seated in beautifully carved pews. In the altar are the bones of the Church Father St. John Chrysostom, Patriarch of Constantinople (350-407), one of the four bishops standing beneath the *Cathedra Petri*. On the altar is the mosaic version of a Pietro Bianchi painting, the Immaculate Conception (1740), a favorite theme of 18th century art. The cut diamonds of the halo are only imitation: the authentic stones are now shown in the Museum of St. Peter's.

Diagonally opposite the Chapel of the Choir and high up on the wall is the bronze tomb of Innocent VIII Cybo (1484-92), the only one in the upper church to come from Old St. Peter's. Cast by Antonio del Pollaiolo in 1498, it shows the Pope twice: below he is lying on his death bed in eternal sleep, as had been the custom so far, and above, for the first time in art history, he is majestically sitting on his throne wearing the tiara. He carries the point of a lance, alluding to the holy lance of Longinus, which he had received as a gift from the Turkish Sultan Bajazet. The pope is surrounded by the allegories of the four cardinal virtues, a theme that Pollaiolo had developed in great style on the monument for Sixtus IV, which we shall see in the Museum.

Opposite is the standing figure of Pius X Sarto (1903-14) by Pier Enrico Astori (1923). The triumphal tiara he is wearing hardly befits this modest and holy Pope. In any case, this is the last time that a Pontiff will be portrayed on his funeral monument with a tiara on his head. His successor Benedict XV della Chiesa (1914-22) has it at his feet, while the others, from Pius XI onwards, simply wear the bishop's mitre.

To the right, at this point, is the Chapel of the

65

65. The Baptismal Font. *In 1695, Carlo Fontana built the Baptistry Chapel, and with it, after nearly 200 years, construction work on New St. Peter's was finished. Every native Roman can be baptized in the font, a Roman porphyry basin (4 × 2 metres) from Castel Sant'Angelo, used for over 600 years as the cover of the sarcophagus of the German Emperor Otto II (d. 983). Fontana enhanced it as baptismal font by giving it an elegant gilded bronze cover.*

Presentation. According to legend, the Virgin Mary as a young girl was taken to the Temple in Jerusalem by her parents to be educated there as a temple Virgin. This event is not mentioned in the Gospels, only in the so-called "Protoevangelium of James", about 200 A.D., but it is commemorated by the liturgy (November 21) and found in Church iconography. The scene portrayed here is the mosaic copy of a painting by Francesco Giovanni Romanelli (1622), now in Santa Maria Maggiore. In the altar itself lies the bronze-covered body of St. Pius X, while in the right-hand corner of this chapel is the monument to John XXIII, a bronze high relief on which Emilio Greco (1970) has represented the Pope's acts of mercy and his opening of the Vatican Council.

To the left of the altar is the monument of Benedict XV by Pietro Canonica. The Pope is shown kneeling, and in the background motifs one can discern allusions to the horrors of World War I, during his pontificate.

Now comes the entrance to the roof, above which two child angels dangle chubby legs and play with a sceptre and crown. These form part of the monument of Mary Clementine Stuart (1702-35), the

granddaughter of the great Polish king John III Sobiesky, the savior of Vienna. Despite the opposition of the heads of state, she married James III, the "older Pretender", son of the last Catholic Stuart king, in exile from England with his father since childhood, and living in Rome. The sarcophagus bears the proud inscription: "Queen of Great Britain, Ireland and France"; but in fact Mary Clementine, like her peers buried in St. Peter's, was a queen without a realm and had never set foot in any of these countries. Consumed with jealousy, perhaps not without good reason, she spent her life in prayer and penance, which soon exhausted her. "When she died, the eyes of the entire Catholic world wept", to quote the pompous words of a funeral orator. Her sepulchre, in the late Baroque style, is by Filippo Barigioni (1745).

The last Stuart Queen left two young sons, Charles Edward, Duke of Albany, and Henry, Duke of York, bishop of Frascati, later archpriest of St. Peter's and finally Cardinal. For these two and for their father, James III, Canova sculpted the monument (1811-19) in the style of an antique pagan stele, which stands opposite that of their unhappy mother and wife. Two angels of death are standing at the entrance to the tomb, mourning over the extinction of the great royal Stuart line.

Our visit to the church of St. Peter concludes with the Baptistry, built in 1695, almost 200 years after the foundation was laid, in 1506. The architect, Carlo Fontana, a nephew of the Domenico Fontana who a century earlier had erected the obelisk in St. Peter's Square and completed the cupola, finished this last chapel. He also did the design for the huge, precious gold-bronze cover of the baptismal font. The porphyry basin is antique, and served for centuries as the sarcophagus of the German Emperor Otto II (d. 983). Particularly remarkable is the mosaic centerpiece of the Baptism of Jesus, from a painting by Carlo Maratta (18th century).

Once the Baptistry had been completed, only a few statues of saints and tombs of popes were added to St. Peter's. Now all of the doors are cast in bronze, each chapel has its altar, and no niche lacks its statue. Only on the side walls is there room left for new medallions of holy popes, which future years will surely bring.

66

The Cupola

66. Tambour of the cupola and detail of the church roof. *To either side of the* Cupolone *are the two minor cupolas by della Porta and one of Maderno's six small cupolas. The stairway leading to the roof of St. Peter's ends in the tile-roofed structure.*

Having now visited the church, one can use the lift to the right of the Baptistry to get to the roof, or go on foot up the 145 step spiral staircase and read on the way the tablets commemorating the Holy Years and the visits of famous people. One's first impression, coming out onto the roof of the church, 45 meters above the ground, is that of being transported into a grey, almost lunar landscape. The ground is sloping and irregular, with the large and small protruding domes of the cupolas and lanterns covered in lead, and with unexpected dips and holes corresponding to the skylights. There are also small turrets, refreshment rooms and souvenir shops. The great bulk of Michelangelo's cupola, the *Cupolone*, seems suddenly quite near us, almost terrifying. To

either side of it are the two smaller cupolas built by Giacomo Della Porta between 1585 and 1590. They have, however, no reference to the church's interior, but stand there simply to enhance and accompany the *Cupolone*, to keep it from seeming solitary in its majestic greatness. Under the sun the dome glimmers from ivory-white to gray, from golden-yellow to rose. At night it withdraws into a magic twilight, except for high feastdays when it is illuminated to a brilliant white by powerful spotlights.

First, as we walk round the terrace, we can look between the gigantic figures (5.70 m) of Christ, the Baptist and the eleven Apostles (i.e. excluding Peter) down to St. Peter's Square below, and then along Via della Conciliazione as far as Castel Sant'Angelo and the bridge across the Tiber. To the north of St. Peter's we can see the whole complex of Apostolic Palaces with courtyards, towers and long galleries extending to the *Palazzetto del Belvedere*. Beyond, on Italian ground, is Monte Mario with its astronomical observatory.

Parallel to St. Peter's stands a rectangular building in reddish brick with walkways and loopholes, conceived as a fortress for the defense of the Vatican. But Sixtus IV wanted to combine religious and military requirements and so turned one floor of the fortress into a papal court chapel. From him, it took the name ''Sistine Chapel''.

In the opposite direction, towards the South, one can see the *Piazza dei Protomartiri Romani* (Square of the first Roman Martyrs), site of Nero's circus, in the center of which the obelisk originally stood (the spot is marked on the pavement). The area of cypresses indicates the *Campo Santo Teutonico*, the Teutonic Cemetery surrounded by the Teutonic College. Behind it, the white convex roof of the Audience Hall is visible. To the right is the Canon's House and the Sacristy, behind the Hospice of St. Martha. Further to the right is St. Martha's Square, surrounded by a number of office buildings and lodgings. But, for a view of the whole of Vatican City, including government offices, railway station, gardens, towers and radio masts, museums and the commercial quarter, one has to climb up even higher, to the top of the dome. Then one can see this tiny state in its entirety on the slope of Vatican Hill, surrounded by walls in the shape of a trapezium 1045 m long at its longest point and 850 m wide at its widest. It is a real state in miniature, the smallest in the world, only 0.44 sq. km in area, ''just big enough to keep body and soul together'', as Pius XI explained when the Vatican State was founded in 1929.

From the roof 16 steps lead inside the cupola. At the entrance to the staircase is the bust of Michelangelo, the copy of an original by Daniele da Volterra. The inscription beneath the bust is taken from the *Motu Proprio* of Paul III, 1549, in which the Pope comments that Michelangelo wanted no reward for building St. Peter's but worked ''out of pure love and special veneration for this basilica''.

By means of a dimly-lit semicircular corridor we come to the interior of the cupola and are able to see over a parapet down into the church. At this point we are at the foot of the tambour, at a height of 53 m from the floor. The diameter of the cupola here is about 43 m (the estimates vary slightly), a little smaller than that of the Pantheon.

67.   The Cupola. *Michelangelo worked to complete this dome until his last days. In his* Life of Michelangelo, *Giorgio Vasari described it in detail and gave the measurement of its every part ''to check the will of the mean-spirited individuals desirous of changing it''. He continues, ''[the cupola] is so clever and well-conceived, and so well-built, that those who know and understand will be unable to see anything more graceful, more beautiful and more well-artificed. This excellence lies in the binding and joining of its stones, in its containing strength and eternity in its every part, in the wisdom used in eliminating rainwater through its many hidden channels, and in its attainment of such perfection that all other structures seen and built until this day are nothing beside the greatness of this one; and it is a great pity that he who had it in his power to have this beautiful and awesome structure vaulted before death could carry away so exceptional a man, did not do so''.*

Now we can see the cupola mosaics up close. Beneath the parapet is a Latin inscription with the words Christ spoke to St. Peter: TU ES PETRUS... ''You are Peter, and upon this Rock I will build my Church'' (Matthew 16, 18-19). Below that are the four Evangelists portrayed in 8.5 m medallions. To give some idea of their scale, one needs only to note that the pen St. Mark is writing with is 1.5 m long. Looking up, we see in six circles ranged towards the apex of the cupola, holy popes and Fathers of the Church; above them, Christ with the Virgin Mary, the Baptist, St. Paul and the Apostles; higher still, angels, Cherubim and Seraphim; and, at the top of the lantern, God the Father with arms outstretched in the act of blessing the created world. All these brilliant mosaics in blue and gold were made from sketches by Cavalier d'Arpino, Cesare Nebbia and Giovanni Guerra in the course of the late 16th and the 17th century.

Giacomo Della Porta and Domenico Fontana built the vault of the dome in 22 months, from July 1588 to May 1590, with a work force of 800 men who worked on a shift system day and night under the baking hot sun or by the light of torches. It was a record-breaking effort which actually required less time and money than the original estimate. As the work had been completed on the initiative of Sixtus V who, like Julius II, had been fired by the ''holy zeal to build'', his name was inscribed high up in the ring of the lantern: S. PETRI GLORIAE SIXTUS PP. V. A. MDXC. PONTIF. V. (To the glory of St. Peter, Sixtus V, 1590, in the 5th year of his pon-

69

68

68.   View from the lantern, towards the *Gover-natorato (west). Further back: Ethiopian College, Leonine Walls with St. John's Tower, radio station and, (right) Fountain of the Eagle.*

69.   View from the lantern, towards the Sistine Chapel (north-east). *To the north, parallel with St. Peter's, a saddle-roofed building containing the Sistine Chapel; to its left the Borgia Tower, anf further off, the Apostolic Palaces.*

tificate). For this cupola, with its lantern, 16.63 m high on top, Michelangelo was not inspired by the Pantheon, as Bramante was, but by Brunelleschi's cupola for the Duomo in Florence.

The outer vault of St. Peter's cupola is not a hemisphere as it is inside but is raised 4 to 7 m above the inner vault, almost like a gothic arch. Whether this was Michelangelo's intention or not is still a matter of debate. Those who hold that the hemisphere is the perfect form, a form which the Renaissance, and therefore Michelangelo, wanted to take up from antiquity, criticize what they consider to be Giacomo Della Porta's arbitrary deviation: for he has given to the dome, perhaps for static reasons, a somewhat gothic profile, more reminiscent of the Middle Ages. But it is precisely this slight swing upwards which gives the cupola its unique beauty. In fact, the same profile is to be found in Michelangelo's wooden model (1558-61) now on exhibition in the Vatican Museums (but it may have been altered), as well as in various sketches of his (one, dated 1548, was recently discovered in the archives of the *Fabbrica*). In addition, there is not a single document in the archives in which mention is made of any alterations to the cupola. Therefore, it is the general view that

70

Michelangelo would have completed it in this form had he lived long enough. As he himself once put it: "because in building, experience will indicate the next step".

The tambour, 20 m high, is decorated on the outside with 16 double Corinthian columns, between which 16 large windows let in the bright light that fills the cupola. On the plinth above the columns, there should have been statues of 16 prophets for which Bernini had already made some designs, but they were never made, for fear they would be too heavy. Above the columns is an attic decorated with garlands of pear branches and heads of lions, a reference to the emblem of Sixtus V, who commissioned the work. In continuation of the columns are 16 vaulting ribs tapering off towards the top and leading the eye to the lantern. Here the features of the tambour are repeated: the lantern is surrounded by double columns, this time, however, in the Ionic style, and topped by 16 so-called candelabra with no function but that of decoration. Between the two spherical vaults of the cupola itself, the internal and the external, a narrow spiral stairway of 302 steps leads to the lantern. At its foot, at a height of 120 m, there is a narrow exterior balustrade from which one

71

70. View from the lantern, towards the Tiber (east). *From the bottom: roof of the central nave, St. Peter's Square, Via della Conciliazione, Castel Sant'Angelo, Ponte Sant'Angelo, and Rome.*

71. View from the lantern, towards the Teutonic Cemetery (south). *From the left: Palace of the Holy Office, Teutonic College and Cemetery, Hall of Audiences. To the right, Sacristy.*

72

73

has a magnificent view of the whole of Rome with its many domes, large and small, round and oval, all trying to emulate the *Cupolone* of St. Peter's. The Sabine mountains are visible to the east, the Alban hills towards southeast, while in the southwest lies the silvery stretch of water which is the Tyrrhenian Sea.

In the past it was possible to go on even further, up a steep staircase, and into the gilded bronze orb, which has a diameter of 2.4 m and was big enough to take 16 people at a time. But now the staircase has been closed for safety reasons. An outside ladder — for the use of the *sampietrini* only — leads to the white metal cross, 3.4 m tall. The distance from the floor of the Grottoes to the very top of the cross is 136.61 m. St. Peter's is not at all the highest church, but, with its full length of 211.50 m, it is the largest church in the world. And because of the unique beauty of its cupola, it has become the symbol of Rome and of the Church at large.

72. Wooden model of the cupola (exterior). *(1558-61). Michelangelo made several models for St. Peter's, but the only surviving one is the fourth, showing the cupola alone, now in the Vatican Museums. Giacomo della Porta is believed to have modified the real outer shell later. Two clues point to his deviation from the model: the pear branch festoon motifs at the base of the dome and the three mounds in a pyramid at the base of the ribs, clear allusions to the emblem of Sixtus V Peretti, who ordered the cupola vaulted. Also the candelabra around the cusp could not have been Michelangelo's idea, for he had planned to place 16 statues of Prophets on the moulding above the columns; and although some were prepared by Bernini, they were never put in place.*

73. Wooden model of the cupola (interior). *This picture makes evident the two shells of the cupola, each with its own structure: the inner shell is a perfect hemisphere, while the outer shell in section is a slightly pointed arch. The diameter of the real cupola at the base of the drum is 43 metres inside, and 59 metres outside. The cupola measures about 90 metres from its base to the top of the cross.*

74. The lantern of the cupola. *Responsability is attributed to della Porta for lowering the lantern to balance his raising the dome's outer shell, and for in-* *creasing the height of the cusp, all deviations from Michelangelo's original plan. The lantern was built in 1591.*

75

The Museum

At the end of the left-hand side-nave, beneath the monument to Pius VIII, a winding corridor — where we can read, on a large tablet, the names of the 147 popes buried in St. Peter's — leads to the Sacristy, a rounded and domed building by Carlo Marchionni (1776-84). Next to it is the entrance to the Art and History Museum of St. Peter's, which houses the

75. Tomb of Sixtus IV. *A "manifesto" of the Christian Renaissance by Antonio del Pollaiolo (1493). Emblematic of the new spirit is the mythological allegory of Theology as* ars venandi Deum *(the art of hunting God) at the side of the Pope's head.* — 76. The Sacristy — 77. The Holy Column, *or Column of the Obsessed, because exorcisms were practiced under it.* — 78. The Crux Vaticana. — 79. Angel. *A clay model by Bernini for the Chapel of the Blessed Sacrament.* — 80. Dalmatic (back), *of the 11th century.* — 81. Sarcophagus of Junius Bassus, *detail.* — 82. *Cock from Old St. Peter's, 9th century.*

76

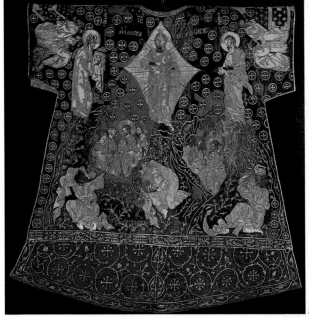

80

81

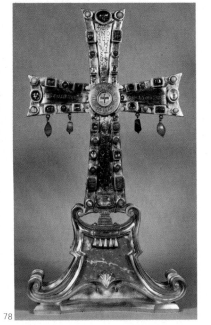

78

77   79

82

treasures assembled in the course of centuries, all charitable donations, unfortunately plundered many times over by the Saracens (846), the German Lansquenets (1527) and French soldiers (1798-1814). The Museum was arranged in 1975 along the most modern lines.

In the first room stands a beautiful twisted column in white Parian marble. This is one of the twelve columns that surrounded the tomb of Peter in the old basilica. This particular one was venerated as the "Holy Column" and was said to have come from the Temple of Solomon in Jerusalem, where Christ had leaned against it when he preached in the Temple and cast out demons.

A bronze cock is the only other object in the room. It stood on the bell-tower of the ancient basilica.

Next comes the room of the *Cathedra Petri*. It contains a facsimile (made in 1974 in the Museum of Mainz, Germany) of the old wooden throne, manufactured in the art school of the Carolingian court at Metz. For centuries it was used as a papal throne. Probably, at the end of the 12th century, 18 plates of ivory were added to the lower front part of the chair, plates which the most recent research claims to have come from a pagan imperial throne belonging to Constantine. They represent the twelve labors of Hercules and six monsters.

Opposite the throne is the "Dalmatic of Charlemagne", a ceremonial tunic which the Emperor was supposed to have worn for liturgical rites. But it is in fact a Byzantine embroidery dating from the 11th century. Here too is the oldest treasure of the Museum, the *Crux Vaticana*, a gift to Rome from Emperor Justin II (d. 578), whose portrait with his wife and *socia*, Sofia, is to be found on the back of the cross-piece.

Next to this room, in a chapel called *Cappella dei Beneficiati*, we see a beautiful tabernacle in marble which Donatello worked on for St. Peter's during his 1432-33 stay in Rome. It contains a very old image of the so-called "Madonna of the Fever", which was invoked for the cure of malaria. In the same chapel we find the mould of Michelangelo's *Pietà*, cast by Francesco Mercatali in 1934. Thanks to this copy, it was possible to restore the original to its exact former state after the act of vandalism that damaged it in 1972.

The next room is wholly occupied by the magnificent bronze monument of Sixtus IV, founder of the Sistine Chapel and the Vatican Library. The monument is signed by Antonio del Pollaiolo (1493). The Pope lies on a bed of state clothed in his ceremonial vestments, the papal tiara contrasting with his haggard face. Around him are seven panels with bas-reliefs representing the three theological Virtues (Faith, Hope and Charity) and the four cardinal Virtues (Prudence, Justice, Fortitude and Temperance); and in an outer circle, the Seven Arts of the Trivium and Quadrivium (Grammar, Rhetoric and Dialectic; Arithmetic, Geometry, Music and Astronomy). These are the disciplines which were then taught in the schools, with the newly discovered art of Perspective added here for the first time. These "arts" prepare the way to Philosophy and Theology which occupy, at the Pope's head, the place of honor.

In the room of Reliquaries, which follows, is the painted wooden frame in which the veil of Veronica was preserved until the 18th century, and a casket of rock crystal, made in Cyprus, which originally contained the point of Longinus' lance.

There follows a series of precious silver candelabra (15th-18th century), and two beautifully illuminated 16th-century music manuscripts for the *Cappella Giulia*, so named after Pope Julius II, who in 1513 created this choir, still existing, for the singing of liturgical chant in St. Peter's.

A white angel with mighty wings, kneeling at prayer, is a clay mould of one of Bernini's bronze angels (1667) in the Chapel of the Blessed Sacrament. The sweet expression of the face, brought out by suitable lighting, comes over better than in the finished work.

Now to a gallery containing a large number of monstrances, chalices, reliquaries and vestments, mainly of the 19th century. Here too we can admire the great early 18th-century tiara, studded with precious stones, with which the famous bronze statue of St. Peter inside the church is crowned each year at the feast of Peter and Paul.

A great art treasure of the Museum, in the last room but one, is the sarcophagus of Junius Bassus, a prefect of the "Eternal City" (Rome) who had become a Christian neophite and died in 359. The sarcophagus is in finely worked and polished Parian marble. The front section is divided into ten high-relief panels, with scenes from the Old and New Testament referring to sorrow, death and redemption. Christ is shown here as a young hero, sitting on a throne between Peter and Paul, his feet resting on the vault of heaven, which the God Uranus is stretching out over his head like a sheet. The pagan god, and the harvest scenes on the side of the sarcophagus are reminiscent of Pagan antiquity. The sarcophagus is therefore an extremely important work of art, shows the transition between paganism and the new Christian era.

83

The Grottoes

83. The Polish Chapel. *Built by Antoni Sko-niecki, a Polish clergyman residing in America, it contains a mosaic of the Madonna of Czenstochowa surrounded by reliefs of the most important Polish saints, by Michael Raszyn (1957).*

Under the great church lies another church, called *Le Sacre Grotte Vaticane*, the Sacred Grottoes of the Vatican. These are underground areas between the floor of the ancient church, and that of the more recent one, built approximately 3 meters above it. These areas were at one time so damp and dark that they really did look like grottoes and could only be visited by torch or candle-light. In this underground realm of death many important persons have been buried.

Between 1935 and 1950, the Grottoes were transformed into a real lower church and equipped with electric lighting. A shadowy, twilight illumination is nonetheless maintained in order to preserve the old mystical atmosphere. Access is at the pilaster of Longinus. A low and narrow semicircular corridor passes along the primitive apse of Constantine's

church and corresponds more or less to the semi-annular crypt which Gregory the Great had built around the tomb of Peter (about 600).

On the right-hand side of the corridor is the grated crypt, containing fragments of the marble monument of Paul II Barbo, (1464-71), the builder of the famous *Palazzo Venezia* in Rome. It follows a series of national chapels, dedicated mostly to the "Churches of Silence". The first is the Polish Chapel with the mosaic image of the Black Madonna of Czenstochowa, followed by the Irish Chapel with a modern mosaic representing St. Columban (521-597), the patron saint of Ireland. There is a Chapel for the Czechs which contains the stone coffin of Cardinal Beran, archbishop of Prague (d. 1969), with a fresco of the "*Madonna della Bocciata*", so called because it was defaced by a drunken soldier with a *boccia* or bowling ball. The

84

Lithuanians also have their national chapel, the newest and the last one in the row.

At the center of the semicircular corridor, we reach and almost touch the heart of St. Peter's. Behind a gilded gate is the "Chapel of St. Peter", formerly called the "Clementine Chapel", after Clement VIII who had it magnificently decorated. The chapel is in the form of an inverted cross, in memory of the crucifixion of Peter with his head down. The altar is very old (6th century) but has recently been covered in precious malachite. Behind this altar is an iron gate through which one can see a wall of white pavonazzetto marble with stripes of red porphyry. That is the rear wall of the funeral monument which the Emperor Constantine had built over the earthen grave of the Apostle. We have to think of it as a large block (2.50 m high, 2.75 m wide and 1.50 m deep) with a door in the middle leading to a niche within, the present Niche of the Pallia, which stood precisely above the first earthen grave of Peter. Six twisted columns of white marble linked by bronze screens surrounded the monument. Curtains and oil-lamps hung from the architraves, and four bronze arches connected the four corners of the monument almost like a crown. It was surmounted by a massive gold cross, donated by Constantine and his mother Helen, as was the gold chandelier hanging over the tomb.

The mausoleum stood free and high up in the center of Constantine's basilica. But in about 600 Gregory the Great had the floor-level raised in order to build a crypt behind the tomb, and he then built an altar above it. In time, a second altar was built over the first by Callistus II of Burgundy (1119-24), enshrining the first one by Gregory the Great. And finally in 1594 Clement VIII placed a third one on top of the other two: the present Papal Altar above the Confession.

Along the external wall of the Chapel of St. Peter there is a marvelous marble frieze, recalling the style of the triumphal arches in the Roman Forum. Its Renaissance artist, probably Matteo del Pollaiolo, was the first consciously to imitate their style. The frieze was made for the marble canopy which Sixtus IV ordered in 1474 for the high altar of the ancient basilica. Its five high reliefs represent the life and martyrdom of Peter and Paul.

Opposite the Chapel of St. Peter is a niche with the sepulchre of Pius XII. As he had sponsored the excavations which led to the discovery of the tomb of Peter, he wished to be buried as near to it as possible.

The semicircular corridor suddenly leads to an underground basilica (55.82 × 13.22 m), divided into three naves by low pilasters. In the southern side-nave, along the outer wall, are several tombs: first, the bright white marble coffin of Pius XI in a niche all decorated with shiny mosaics. He is the pope who in 1929 signed the Lateran Treaties, which sealed the reconciliation between Church and State in Italy and engendered the new Vatican City State. In the following niche we see an iron crown set upon a sarcophagus. It is the crown of England which the exiled King James III (d. 1776), never had the chance to wear. He is resting here beside his two sons, Charles Edward, Duke of Albany (d. 1778), and Cardinal Henry, Duke of York (d. 1807), the last Stuarts, whose monument by Canova we saw in the upper church. Next follows the tomb of Innocent XIII (1721-24) of the noble Conti family, to which two other popes (Innocent II and Alexander IV) belonged; then the tomb of Urban VI Prignano (1378-89), whose election, the first after the return of the popes from Avignon, caused a schism in the Church for almost 40 years.

Alongside these are, two empty tombs: that of Callistus III Borgia (1455-58), and that of Pius III Todeschini-Piccolomini (1503), both of them removed to other Roman churches.

The only English pope in history was Hadrian IV Breakspeare (1154-59). As a child he went begging. As pope, he crowned the mighty Emperor Frederick I

85

84. S. Peter's Chapel. *It is also called the Clementine Chapel for Clement VIII, who had it enlarged and decorated in about 1600. Its location corresponds to the crypt that Gregory I built to allow the faithful to pray beside St. Peter's tomb. In fact, it penetrates the apse of Old St. Peter's radially as far as the Constantinian monument (cfr. 85 and 93).*

85. Reconstruction of the Constantinian Monument. *At the center of the apse of Old St. Peter's, Constantine built a mausoleum to enclose and exhalt the 2nd century* aedicula *over the Saint's sepulchre.*

Barbarossa. He is at rest here in a heavy antique sarcophagus of granite.

At the far end of this nave we can see (but not get close to) the German Chapel, containing the mortal remains of three Germans: Emperor Otto II, who died in Rome in 983 at the age of only 28, and his nephew, who as Gregory V (996-999) was the first of five German popes. Between them the prelate Ludwig Kaas (1881-1952) lies buried underground. As director of the *Fabbrica di San Pietro*, he was responsible for the excavations and the reconstruction of the Grottoes. Above the altar in the center, a 10th-century mosaic shows Christ between Peter and Paul. Peter does not carry two keys, as he usually does, but three, symbolizing perhaps the three powers of the

86

church — to minister, to teach, to govern — or the Church as militant on earth, penitent in purgatory and triumphant in heaven.

We are now in the central nave, in front of a marble arch, closed by a great glass window, through which we can now see directly into the *Confession* and the Niche of the Pallia. Above the arch an inscription reads: SEPULCRUM SANCTI PETRI APOSTOLI, because the niche stands above the original earthen grave of Peter, and to the right is the wall containing the remains of the Apostle.

The kneeling marble statue of Pius VI Braschi (1775-89), Canova's last work (1822), which up to now stood in front of Peter's tomb in the Confes-

sion, has been removed to the opposite end of the middle nave, still facing the Confession. He died, a prisoner of Napoleon, in France. His body was brought back to Rome and buried next to Peter's tomb in an early Christian sarcophagus, the first to the left in the third and last nave. On the altar next to it is a lovely marble relief, ''The Madonna of the Orsini Family'', sculpted by Isaia da Pisa in the 15th century for the Orsini Chapel of Old St. Peter's.

In this northern nave we find the tombs of the last popes: first, John XXIII, the Pope of Vatican Council II and ecumenism. He rests in a simple sarcophagus above which is a relief of a Madonna with Child and two Angels: the Madonna has peasant,

87

86. **The Crucifixion of Peter.** *A detail from a Renaissance relief, perhaps by Matteo del Pollaiolo. Peter may have been crucified with his head downward as tradition has it, but John (21, 18) just implies that he was crucified, and historians claim only that he was executed in Nero's circus.*

87. **The German Chapel.** *On the front wall, fragments from Matilda of Canossa's donation act giving her goods to the Church (1102). The title on the sarcophagus of Otto II, to the left, is "Imperator Augustus". In fact, he was crowned in St. Peter's, at the age of twelve.*

maternal features, and was probably sculpted by Luigi Capponi (16th century).

Near Pope John's tomb two queens are also buried. One is Christina of Sweden, whose great monument in the upper church we have already seen. The other is the last Queen of Cyprus, Carola Lusignan-Savoy (1442-87), who was expelled from her island and spent the rest of her life at the papal court with her picturesque Greek-Oriental retinue.

Down two steps now and we are on the right of the tomb of Benedict XV, who was pope at the time of the First World War. Through a number of openings under this tomb (the work of Giuliano Barbieri), one can see down into the antique cemetery.

The next tomb is that of John Paul I Luciani

(Aug.-Sept. 1978), who in only 33 days of papacy conquered the affection of the entire world. It is a sarcophagus in grey marble with two Renaissance angels at the corners. Opposite are the tombs of Innocent IX Facchinetti (Nov.-Dec. 1591) and Marcellus II Cervini (April-May 1555), to whom Palestrina dedicated his famous *Missa Papae Marcelli*.

Lying flat on the floor of the next niche is the travertine tombstone of Paul VI Montini (1963-78), who wished to be buried in plain earth with neither flowers or candles. There is only a relief on the wall, of previously existing 15th-century Madonna with Child. In fact the tombs of the popes are evidence of how the concept of the papacy has changed since the time of the Renaissance, becoming more spiritualized after centuries of pomp and temporal power. After the tomb of Julius III Ciocchi del Monte (1550-55), there is an arrow pointing to the exit round the corner. If we wanted to see the remaining part of the Grottoes, we would have to ask for a special pass from the "*Fabbrica*". We could then visit the tombs of Innocent VII Migliorati (1404-06), of Nicholas V Parentucelli (1447-55), the first Humanist to occupy the papal chair, and of Boniface VIII, who in 1300 announced the first Holy Year, and in 1302 issued the famous bull *Unam Sanctam*. Arnolfo di Cambio, the probable sculptor of the statue of Peter in the upper church, has portrayed

him lying on his death-bed above a finely pleated marble sheet. On the right is an old sarcophagus which contains the bones of Nicholas III Orsini (1277-80), a pope whom we saw kneeling at the feet of the "Madonna of the Orsini Family".

At the far end of this northern side-nave we can just make out in the half-light a frescoed Madonna by Lippo Memmi, called "Madonna of the Bombardment" because it was damaged by a bomb which fell on the Vatican in November 1943, during the last world war. The Madonna was in the Mosaic Studio, which was caught by fragments of the explosion.

Several side-rooms not open to the public are filled with interesting fragments from Old St. Peter's, among which the beautiful sarcophagus of Anicius Probus, 395, brought to safety here before the demolition of the ancient basilica. Now we approach the exit, near which is a niche where St. Peter the Apostle is sitting lifesized in marble. It is an antique Roman copy of a Greek original, representing a pagan philosopher, found in the Borgo, near St. Peter's. In 1565 the sculptor Nicolò de Longhi da Viggiù was commissioned to transform the pagan statue into a Saint Peter, by putting a new head on it with curly beard and halo. His left hand also was ex-

88.   Statue of Pius VI. *This piece by Canova (1822), formerly in the Confession and now at the end of the Grottoes, has on its base the humble inscription "Pius VI Braschi, from Cesena. Pray for him".*

89.   St. Peter in the Grottoes. *This classical pagan statue, found in the* Borgo *long ago, was made into an image of St. Peter by Niccolò Longhi da Viggiù in 1565. For centuries hidden in the Grottoes it now stands in evidence near the exit.*

changed for a new one carrying the keys of Peter instead of a scroll. The statue, which had an honorable place in the atrium of the old St. Peter's, was the model for the new bronze statue of St. Peter in the upper church. Now we find ourselves in one of the many courtyards of the Vatican, on the northern side of the church, at the foot of the Sistine Chapel. From here we can return to the entrance hall of St. Peter's.

90

The Excavations beneath St. Peter's

90. Road (*iter*) of the Necropolis. *Between 1941 and 1949, seventy metres of an ancient necropolis beneath St. Peter's were brought to light. It had been buried by Constantine, who wanted his basilica built exactly above St. Peter's tomb.*

Below the Vatican's Sacred Grottoes we can visit the ancient necropolis, seven meters under the present church (having first obtained permission from the *Ufficio Scavi*, the Excavation Office). Emperor Constantine had it buried in about 320, so as to level the site on which the church was going to be built exactly over the tomb of Peter. Only an Emperor could dare such an undertaking and only for very impelling reasons, for otherwise it would have constituted a sacrilege against the Roman cult of the dead. The cir-

91

cumstance itself speaks for the authenticity of St. Peter's tomb on this very spot. It had already happened that while digging the foundations of the second church in the 16th century, workmen had come across some ancient tombs, but out of fear and reverence no one dared to explore further. Yet the Romans had always been convinced that the tomb of Peter was beneath the high altar of his church. The papal commission instituted by Pius XII in 1939 affirmed the old Roman tradition when it actually found the tomb of Peter, precisely where it was believed to be.

Access to the excavations is from the south side of the church. First we pass through three rooms full of remains of Constantine's building, until we reach the outside walls of the ancient basilica. A few steps down bring us suddenly into an underground world. This necropolis was probably one of the largest in Rome and extended from east to west. But only 70 meters of it have been excavated, as far as was necessary to reach from the site of the Chapel of the Blessed Sacrament to the papal altar. On two sides of a narrow street (*iter*) there are 22 funeral chambers, with frescoed walls, mosaic or marble flooring, windows and entrance doors.

The majority of the families buried here belonged to the well-to-do middle class of merchants, civil servants and freedmen who had made their fortunes. The mausolea were pagan in origin, as may be inferred from the various symbols and, in a free syncretism, we find Greek and Roman gods beside oriental and Egyptian divinities. Later on, some members of these families became Christian — as proved by the expressions *deposito and deponere*, meaning to put away and preserve until the resurrection. They were buried nonetheless with their pagan relatives. The time of the greatest expansion of the necropolis was the 2nd century. But some of the tombs go back to the time of Peter, while others reach the age of Constantine. The first Mausoleum (A) at the lower, east end of the street, still bears the *titulus* over the door (this was a marble slab giving the owner's name and, occasionally, his social standing, age and other information). This 2nd century mausoleum belongs to Popilius Heracla. The *titulus* states that he had required his heir to build him a funeral monument "*in Vaticano ad Circum*". If the heir had not complied with this clause, he certainly would not have mentioned it. Thus we have a written confirmation that the necropolis was near the cir-

92

91. Mausoleum B (2nd century). *Delicate frescoes with musical instruments, flowers and peacocks, symbols of immortality (left-hand border of the photo) decorate the walls, which have niches for cinerary urns and arcosolia for sarcophagi.*

92. Mosaic with Christ-the-Sun. (Mausoleum of the Julii, 3rd century). *At the center of a mosaic ceiling with vine shoots, symbol of the Church, is Christ as radiant Sun God riding a quadriga.*

cus, extending to its right-hand (northern) boundary, along the far side of the street which led to the circus itself. At that time, the dead were actually buried along the roads outside the city walls.

If we continue, we see to our right the Mausoleum of Marcia and the Mausoleum (Z), called Mausoleum of the Egyptians, owing to a mural painting of the Egyptian god of death, Horus. In both of these, there are fine sarcophagi with Dionysian scenes symbolizing eternal bliss.

Opposite is the Mausoleum of the Caetennii (F) which contains the tomb of a Christian woman, Aemilia Gorgonia. On the wall, she is depicted standing before a fountain, taking water with an amphora. Next to this design, are the words: *Anima dulcis Gorgonia*, sweet soul Gorgonia. Water is the early Christian popular symbol for the *refrigerium*, a cool and refreshing place, as the Christians in the hot countries imagined heaven to be.

The magnificent neighbouring Mausoleum (H) of the Valerii is the largest of all. Divinities of different cults are depicted in elegant stucco-work. In a wall niche are two heads roughly drawn in charcoal. One could be Christ; the other, bald and ugly, is supposed to be Peter, owing to the Latin words scrawled alongside it: "Peter, pray for the holy Christian folk buried near your body". These are amazing words. If the reading is correct, they prove that the man who wrote them around 300 was sure that he was in the immediate vicinity of Peter's tomb.

Squeezed in the narrow space between two pagan tombs is the 3rd century Christian sepulchre of the Julii (M). Perhaps the Julii chose this position, not in itself a propitious one, so as to be near the tomb of Peter, as many Christians longed to be. The Mausoleum is very small, but of considerable interest, as it contains almost all the early symbols of Christ: the Good Shepherd, the Mystical Fisherman, and Jonah, who for three days was in the belly of the whale, as Jesus was in the realm of the dead. The whole ceiling is covered with mosaics showing vine branches, another symbol of Christ, the "vine" (John, 15,5). In the center we see Christ rising towards heaven in a quadriga and surrounded by sun beams. This representation of Christ as the True Sun is a new expression of hope in the resurrection, but still in a pagan figuration.

After Mausoleum S, which borders on "Field P" at the rear, the underground alley turns to the right. We come to a long narrow wall, called the "Red Wall" because of the red color of its plaster surface. Behind it a narrow path (*clivus*) leads upwards from south to north to further funeral chambers higher up. Under this *clivus* is a drainage ditch to eliminate the water flowing down the hillside. Trademarks can still be made out on the bricks covering this small channel. Fortunately, the bricks were made in a factory belonging to two well-known personalities: *Aurelius Caesar* and *Faustina Augusta*. They therefore date back to the period in which Marcus Aurelius was only *Caesar* and not yet *Augustus*, while his wife already had the title of *Augusta*, that is between 147 and 161. Thus, we have a date for both the *clivus* and the "Red Wall" (obviously built together). The "Red Wall" was to protect and mark

62

The Excavations beneath St. Peter's

from behind the boundary of a specific sepulchre. But which sepulchre?

To discover this we must reach the front of the "Red Wall", by climbing back up to the Chapel of St. Peter, and then going through a door on the right and down some steps again. There we find a brick wall, which belongs to the funeral monument which Constantine had built over the tomb of Peter. We have already seen the marble rear wall of the monument through the Chapel of St. Peter. Now we can also see traces of the bronze screens, and the base of the marble column which surrounded the mausoleum. In order to find out what was behind the wall, the excavation team broke through the brickwork and discovered a small white marble column (80 cm high) still fixed in the wall, and supporting a travertine slab (1.75 × 0.50 m) resting against the "Red Wall". Thanks to it the experts were able to reconstruct the shape and size (2.70 × 1.75 m) of the first little monument which (as revealed by the age of the marks stamped on the bricks of the *clivus*) was built around the year 160, over the earthen tomb of Peter. It had the shape of a small house (*aedicula*) with two niches, the larger of which later became the famous Niche of the Pallia. This must have been the monument mentioned by the *presbyter* Gaius around 200 in a polemical letter to Proclus, a leader of the Montanist sect: "But I can show you the tombs of the Apostles, because if you come to the Vatican or along the *Via Ostiensis*, you'll be able to see the trophies (*tropaia*) of the founders of the community" (Eusebius, *History of the Church*, 2,25, 5-7). Gaius referred to the sepulchre with the Greek word "trophy" because the death of a martyr means victory of faith and life over death. The sepulchre was also called *Locus Petri* or *Memoria Petri*. During the 2nd century a courtyard was developed in front of the *tropaion*. The courtyard, now termed "P Camp" by the experts, is about 8 × 4 m. A mosaic floor was added later, thus proving that this tomb was always kept with care, also in the following centuries.

Towards the middle of the 3rd century, a strange wall was built on the right side, north of the *aedicula* and perpendicular to the "Red Wall", upsetting the symmetry of the complex. It is 86 cm long and 45 cm thick. Its original height is not known because its upper part was demolished when the wall was included in the Constantinian burial monument. It is called "Wall g" because of the *graffiti* covering its outside. This wall is of particular importance. To find out why, we have to return to the Chapel of St. Peter and go through the door on the left. Now that we are fac-

ing the right-hand (north) side of the monument, we can see where the Constantinian protecting wall was broken through by the excavators and, behind it, the famous "Wall g", covered with the mysterious code writing used by the early Christians. There are exclamations hailing Christ, Mary and Peter, and invocations for the living and the dead. Of special interest are the words *hoc vince*, scribbled on the wall by an unknown hand together with the monogram of Christ . They mean "with this sign go and win!" They were the exact words which the Emperor Constantine claimed to have heard on the night before the decisive battle at Milvian Bridge, on October 28, 312, which brought about his victory over Maxentius, and that of Christianity over paganism. The graffito must have been scratched on there shortly after that extraordinary event: hence, in 312 the wall still must have been accessible. But soon after that, the Emperor had the aedicola of 160, along with "Wall g", walled up in an even larger monument, and so he hid the tomb and the graffiti. But first he had a hollow space knocked out of "Wall g" and had it covered on the inside with five fine slabs of marble, like an urn (77 × 29 × 31 cm) without a lid. We can now look through this irregular-shaped aperture to the inside of the marble urn and see a number of whitened bones. Are these the relics of the Apostle Peter? How can we be sure of it?

When archaelogist Margherita Guarducci discovered these bones on September 25, 1953, she had no idea that what she had found were the long-sought-after mortal remains of the Prince of the Apostles. She made sure, nonetheless, that the contents of the urn were thoroughly examined by anthropologists, chemists, biologists, numismatists and other specialists. Anthropologist Venerando Correnti reassembled the bones: they turned out to belong to a single individual, a robust male figure in old age. This corresponds to the image of Peter, but is not in itself sufficient evidence. Prof. Correnti simply labelled the skeleton VMG (*Vano Muro g*), which means, the hollow space inside "Wall g". The bones were encrusted with earth, matching that of the original tomb, which the excavators had already discovered directly beneath the Niche of the Pallia, but found empty. Mingled with the bones of VMG were animal bones, evidence that VMG must have been buried when the Vatican hill was still pasture ground, that is the first century A.D. After this date, as we already know, the necropolis developed, and sheep and cattle breeding came to an end.

Red patches were also found on the bones, together

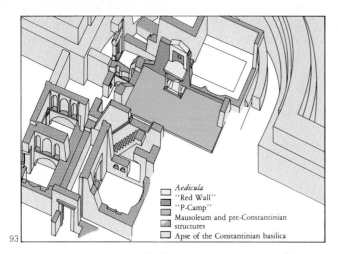

93

94

93. Axonometric projection of the ''P-Camp'' zone. *In the diagram, part of the* iter *among the tombs, and the ''P-Camp'' with the* aedicula *over Peter's first sepulchre against the ''Red Wall'', between 160 and 260. Behind: the apse of the Constantinian basilica.*

94. ''G-Wall'' with the relics of St. Peter. Erected about mid-3rd century, it was covered with graffiti by the faithful come to worship Peter's tomb. Constantine built a loculus in it for the venerated relics removed from the original earthen grave.

Within the diagram legend:
Aedicula
''Red Wall''
''P-Camp''
Mausoleum and pre-Constantinian structures
Apse of the Constantinian basilica

with purple and gold threads. These were analyzed to establish their authenticity and age. It transpired that VMG had been wrapped in a costly purple fabric woven with gold thread before being placed in the urn, a practice used only if the dead person was of exceptional importance. So one must ask: who can this robust, elderly first century man have been, buried with princely honors in the tomb of the Apostle, if not Peter himself? Judging by the cult of the dead in ancient Rome, it is hardly likely that a substitution was made, nor would another person altogether have been knowingly buried in the tomb of the Apostle. There are no other bones, neither in the monument nor in the earthen grave. Nor could the bones of Peter have been secretly removed, because the earthen grave, together with the *aedicula* and ''Wall g'' were walled up and rendered inaccessible until 1940, when the papal commission partly demolished the stone-work in order to reach the tomb.

Anyone who does not regard these circumstantial clues as conclusive, can read written evidence. In the cavity of ''Wall g'' someone, perhaps the man charged with transferring the bones, scratched two Greek words on the red plaster, *Petros eni* (''Peter is in here''). The writer, being aware of the importance of these remains, left us a kind of declaration of authenticity like that often inscribed in the cornerstone of a new building.

When the findings of the various experts had been assessed, on June 26, 1968 Pope Paul VI declared:

''The relics of St. Peter have been identified in such a way that they can be deemed convincing''. The following evening, in a private but solemn ceremony, Paul VI had the bones replaced in the urn which Constantine had intended for them and in which they had remained hidden for more than 1600 years. These relics now lie, carefully classified and subdivided, in the uncovered urn, protected by a wall of plate glass. Anyone who wishes to may see the relics for himself. Perhaps the spectator will then feel himself transported back in time to the age and presence of Christ, whom Peter was allowed to imitate until his identical death on the cross. He may then realize that the tomb of Peter is the foundation stone of the whole church above and that the words of Matthew (16,18), written inside the cupola, are true also in a literal sense: ''You are Peter, the rock, and upon this rock I will build my Church''.

95.

95. Square, Façade and Palace from Via della Conciliazione. *St. Peter's Square and the basilica façade; to the right, the Apostolic Palace with Bramante's Loggias, and, behind, the roof of the Sistine Chapel.*

96. *Back cover:* Carlo Maderno's nave. *This detail is from an oil-painting on canvas by Giovanni Paolo Pannini (1735) at the Norman Simon Foundation in Los Angeles.*